UNDER ONE ROOF

Caring For an Aging Parent

UNDER ONE ROOF

CARING FOR AN AGING PARENT

by

Sheelagh McGurn

Parkside Publishing
205 W. Touhy Avenue
Park Ridge, Illinois 60068-5881

McGurn, Sheelagh
  Under One Roof

ISBN 0-942421-38-8

Printed in the United States of America
10 9 8 7 6 5 4 3 2 1

CONTENTS

PREFACE

During the course of writing this book, I interviewed many people who are or have been in the position of caring for aging parents. I interviewed people of different economic and social backgrounds. I interviewed people whose ages ranged from mid-thirties to early sixties. Some had small children and some had families that were grown and no longer living in the home.

I also chose families whose parent or parents were in different stages of aging and health. Some parents were fairly young and healthy but lonely following the death of a spouse; others were older or more seriously ill.

Each of these families found good points and bad points in the arrangement. All of them said they were not sorry for the decision they made to bring the parents into their homes.

In my case, and that of most of the people I interviewed, the experience of combining households with a parent started with a problem. Perhaps a parent became seriously ill. Maybe one spouse passed away and the other couldn't cope. In some cases, physical deterioration had been slowly taking place and finally the parent could no longer completely take care of himself or herself.

Regardless of how the problem developed, it is a recognized neediness in the parent that usually starts the process of combining homes. Part One of this book addresses possible physical, psychological, and emotional problems you and your family may encounter, and demonstrates how other people have approached these problems.

Part Two addresses the simple but very important aspect of the physical move and the impact this may have on you, your family, and your parents. The process of giving up the parents' apartment or house, shifting everyone around, or building onto your own house can be physically, emotionally, and financially trying. Preplanning is essential to making this process as free of stress as possible.

You will certainly find your situation unique. We have tried, however, to cover as many different types of problems and living arrangements as possible.

Now I would like to introduce you to the people I interviewed and tell you a little bit about them. In each case, I will be introducing the person whose parent is living in the home and explain as best as possible the physical, mental, and emotional state of the parent.

K.H. Kathy is a professional woman in her late thirties. She works full-time in a very high-pressure job. She and her husband, Tom, have two small children and live in a suburb of a large Midwestern city. Kathy is an only child. Kathy's father has lived with her family for 10 years, since the death of his wife—Kathy's mother. Kathy's father is 80 years old and in very good health. Kathy's father basically tends to his own needs. He drives, so he can take himself to any appointments he may need to. He also does most of the family's grocery shopping and drives his grandchildren to some of their extracurricular activities. He is very health conscious and walks every day to stay in shape. He is mentally very alert and has no apparent emotional problems.

S.L. Sara is in her mid-thirties and does not work outside the home. She and her husband, Kevin, have two young daughters. She and her family live in a large city. Sara's mother is now living with Sara's family. Sara is one of four surviving children. This is the second time Sara's mother has moved in with the family. Following the death of Sara's father, Sara's mother felt she couldn't live alone. After living with the family for awhile, and adjusting to the death of her husband, Sara's mother decided to try living on her own. However, after a few years, her health started to slip and she moved back in with Sara. When Sara's mother first lived with Sara's family, she had very few physical problems. She now has a heart condition and severe problems with her legs. Although she can get around to a degree, the problems with her health have also caused her a considerable amount of anxiety. Because she is afraid she will fall or have an attack of angina, she is understandably afraid to be left in the house alone.

P.M. Patrick M. is a police officer in a large Midwestern city. He took his mother in when she became depressed about living alone. Although she had few physical problems, she did have severe emotional problems, and she became "addicted" to hospitals and doctors. She eventually reached the stage of not being happy anywhere but in a hospital. At the time his mother moved in with his family, Patrick had four children living at home ranging in age from 8 to 16. Although the family accepted the living arrangement, his mother was not particularly happy with it and went into a nursing home. Patrick had three sisters all of whom had, at one time or another, taken on the responsibility of caring for their mother.

V.T. Virginia took care of her mother both in her home and while her mother lived alone in apartments. She was geographically closer to her mother than her sisters and brother and automatically assumed the responsibility for her mother. At the time that Virginia was caring for her mother, she had six children living at home and one in a home for the developmentally disabled. The additional time and effort with her mother was a strain on Virginia although her sisters and brother did help as much as they could. Virginia's mother was addicted to prescription drugs although no one, including the mother, realized this. Because of this, she, at times, exhibited what seemed to the family very strange behavior. She would become depressed and had difficulty remembering things. Her stomach was continually upset, but the doctors she was taken to could find nothing wrong with it. She had been referred to many different doctors, most of whom knew nothing of the other doctors. These problems kept Virginia's mother and the rest of the family in a fairly constant state of confusion.

J.M. Jane did not move her mother into her home. She, instead, lived in her mother's home. Jane was unmarried and worked full-time until her mother became a victim of Alzheimer's disease. Her mother's illness progressed to the point at which she could no longer be left alone at all and Jane found it necessary to quit work to care for her. When Jane's mother first started exhibiting the symptoms of Alzheimer's disease, Jane became very confused and angry. She mistook her mother's growing inability to perform simple daily tasks as a deliberate attempt to get attention. As Jane became more familiar with the symptoms of the disease, and learned more about what to expect, she was better able to understand what was happening.

K.V. Karen is one of four children, is married, and has two children. Karen is also a recovering alcoholic raised in an alcoholic family. Karen's father was a practicing alcoholic until his death. Karen's mother, who moved in with Karen and her family after the death of the father, did not drink but was seriously affected by her years in a dysfunctional family. Although Karen's mother's health was failing when she moved in with Karen, it was her mental health that most affected the family. Karen was familiar with the problems of the alcoholic, but was not as aware of the emotional problems faced by those living with the alcoholic. Since Karen's mother had never taken steps to join support groups for the families of alcoholics, she was herself unaware of the damage her life with a practicing alcoholic had caused her.

INTRODUCTION

When my maternal grandfather was in his fifties, he caught a cold. The cold developed into a case of pneumonia. Antibiotics had not yet been developed. As a result, Grandpa died before he ever reached his sixtieth birthday. His family was not yet completely raised. This story was, in the very recent past, not uncommon. Living past sixty-five or seventy was the exception rather than the rule. Of my grandparents, only one grandmother lived long enough for me to get to know and love her.

Today, we are appalled when we hear of people dying in their sixties let alone their fifties. Living well into the seventies and eighties is not at all uncommon anymore. Healthier life-styles coupled with advanced medical techniques have extended the average life expectancy greatly.

Because of this change in longevity, people are becoming more able today to experience living in multi-generational families. Grandparents and even great grandparents are able to share their wealth of knowledge and experience with their families.

Although the vast majority of elderly in our society today are basically healthy and capable of taking care of themselves, there are problems—some big and some small—which do concern the elderly and which have given our society a whole new group of challenges to meet. One of the challenges that many modern families are now facing is the care of aging parents who can no longer, for whatever reason, live on their own.

How This Book Came About

Close to fifteen years ago, my mother-in-law came to live with our family. We had many good times while Grandma lived with us. Although both my husband and I were totally optimistic about having Grandma come to live with us, we ran into some unexpected problems. In our case, many of these problems were related to Grandma's mental and physical health. Often, we were baffled by her behavior such as wandering the house all night or saying she was sick when she wasn't, and by our reactions to her. We were at a loss to know what to do or who to talk to about it. When we talked to her other children, they usually said they had the same problems with her and were equally at a loss to know what to do. At times, we became very frustrated. We were trying our hardest and it didn't seem to be making a difference in Grandma's general happiness. Fifteen or twenty years ago, there were precious few places we could go for help. Grandma eventually ended up in a nursing home before she died.

Almost thirteen years after Grandma died, my mother's health deteriorated to the point that she could no longer cope with daily tasks at home. Rather than suggest a nursing home, we invited my mother and father to come and live with us. Although both my husband and I were totally optimistic about having my parents live with us, we ran into some unexpected problems. Does this sound familiar? We were just as surprised and baffled this time as we had been thirteen years earlier with my mother-in-law. We couldn't understand why, when our intentions were so good, things could go so wrong at times. This got me to thinking about the whole idea of having parents move into an adult child's home and the problems that we had encountered. I was obviously laboring under a misconception when I figured that good intentions automatically guarantee good results. I knew that everyone involved in my family, including my parents, had good intentions. Maybe we were all just losing our minds.

Rather than assume insanity was at the base of our problems, I started to talk to friends and acquaintances who also had their parents living with them. To my great relief, I found that these people—all of whom had the best intentions—also ran into unexpected problems. This book is the result of our experiences and those of others who have had the experience of their parents living with them for one reason or another. It, of course, is not representative of all families or all problems. There are probably families somewhere out there who experienced no problems while in the process of reorganizing their families to include their aging parents, however, I was not able to find any. We all experienced some confusion, some difficulty, and some frustration. We all lived to tell about it though, and basically what we want to tell you is that it can be done and it can be done in such a way that we are all happy with the outcome.

Since all people are different, this book is certainly not describing all elderly people or all problems that might arise with the elderly. That would be an impossible, if not ridiculous, task. We hope only to address possible common situations and offer various approaches to these situations.

The focus of the book is adult children and elderly parents who choose for one reason or another to combine their households and form extended families.

Reasons for Combining Families
Death of a Spouse
One reason given by many people for combining households was the death of a spouse. One spouse passed away and the remaining spouse simply didn't want to live alone. Some widows and widowers who choose not to live alone move to retirement communities. Others, however, choose to

live with an adult child simply because they feel more comfortable in a familiar family setting. This arrangement often benefits everyone involved. This is the situation Kathy, who you will meet in greater detail later, and her father found themselves in. When Kathy's mother passed away, Kathy's father first lived alone in an apartment but then chose to move in with Kathy's family. Kathy's dad is a perfectly healthy, vigorous man who is more than capable of taking care of himself. He does, in fact, take care of himself. He simply chose to live with his family rather than live alone. He enjoys the daily interaction with his daughter, son-in-law, and grandchildren and he is able to help Kathy, who works full-time, around the home. They, in turn, enjoy being able to have him as an integral part of their family. The children know him in a way few grandchildren get to know their grandparents. In Kathy's case, everyone benefits from this living arrangement.

Declining Health

Another reason given by people I talked with was the declining health of the parent or parents. This, in fact, seemed to be the primary reason for families deciding to combine. One or both parents experienced increasing difficulties managing daily tasks in their own homes, so the families decided to combine to help meet those needs.

The needs expressed by the people interviewed for this book ranged from fairly minor lack of ability to keep house or cook to serious mental or physical deterioration. Some families interviewed but not discussed in this book, found that after careful consideration of alternatives, the difficulties being experienced by their parents were easily solved by arranging for varying degrees of in-home services. These services ranged from weekly cleaning help to daily house-keeping and cooking and, in each of these cases, the families found that combining was not, at least at present, necessary. Many of these parents did not exhibit any desire to leave their homes so alternative solutions were worked out.

Since the focus of this book is on families that do combine, other health-care alternatives, such as nursing homes and home health care are only covered as they apply to the families that did decide to combine.

Changing Times

It is important to remember that the stories recounted and the solutions found are pertinent to the people involved at the time of the interviews. As time passes and circumstances change, each family will need to reevaluate its living situation. Elderly parents who are healthy and vigorous today may become frail at some future time. The circumstance would then change drastically. On the other hand, a parent who moves in with an adult child because of illness may improve in health and decide a change is in order.

No set answer can be used in dealing with human beings. We are simply presenting situations, concerns, and possible solutions to problems. Some of these problems and concerns seemed to surface over and over in the interviews. Many, however, were much more specific to health problems exhibited by the parents involved. You may recognize yourself and your parents in some of the stories and not in the others. Hopefully we have covered enough ground to be of help in the situation you and your family find yourselves in.

You and Your Family Are Unique

Your family is unique. The situation you find yourselves in is not unique. Because of this, you will need to use the experiences and suggestions in this book in light of your family situation. As situations change, so must family dynamics.

Living with a physically and emotionally healthy parent is very different from living with a parent who is suffering from physical or emotional problems. I have tried to provide examples of each of these situations and possible problems that may arise. I am not, nor were the people interviewed, gerontologists. We are simply people—untrained for the most part in psychology or health care—who found ourselves in a position to help our parents.

As in any living arrangement, we found some problems and much joy. The care of a seriously ill parent—either physically, mentally, or emotionally—certainly involves a different set of problems and adjustments than living with healthy parents. But we found in all cases, patience and love were the keys to developing new and stronger relationships with the members of our families, no matter what their condition.

Be Open

One thing that stood out throughout the interviews was that we must be open to asking for help. When a healthy parent becomes ill, or a frail parent becomes more frail, we can become overwhelmed by the increased physical demands of caring for a sick person. We may also succumb to the strong emotional responses we may feel when faced by the sickness of a loved one. We are not alone, nor do our parents need to be alone, if faced with increasing physical problems. Many hospitals and social service agencies now offer services to help the elderly cope with physical problems and to stay as healthy as they can for as long as they can. These same agencies quite often offer caretaker support groups that are a great help in dealing with possible problems. These services are available almost anywhere you might live, and the professionals involved can be lifesavers in times of stress-causing emergencies.

Have Faith

If you are considering asking your elderly parent(s) to live with your family, have faith in your basic feelings and instincts. If you feel that it can be done to everyone's satisfaction, it probably can. Don't let transitory problems or confusions dishearten you. Keep in mind that everyone involved has his or her own personality and will need time to adjust. Most of the problems mentioned in this book were separated by long stretches of peace and happiness. Human beings, however, have a tendency to dwell on the problems and forget to dwell on the good times. Even in fairy tales, the heroes have to slay the dragon before they can get to the happily ever after time. Our purpose is to help you slay the dragons so you can get on with the happily ever after part.

1

LIVING UNDER ONE ROOF AGAIN

Throughout high school, my curfew was somewhere around 10:30. My brother and sister and I did not go out during the week, and on weekends we were expected to let my mother know where we were at all times. When I went to college, my curfew changed to midnight. Even after I graduated and started teaching, I was expected in the house no later than 2:00 AM. If I was going to be late, I had to call home. Until the day I moved out of my mother's house, she would wait up for me to come home. We lived in a very small house. The front door opened directly into the living room. I knew that no matter when I walked through the door, whether it was 10:00 PM or 5:00 AM, my mother would be sitting in her chair in the living room waiting. The reception I got upon entering would depend entirely on how late it was. The routine never varied. I was 25 when I moved out.

After I moved out of my parent's house, I assumed that my parents and I would never again be in the position of learning to adjust to each other's ideas of how a home should be run. I would have my home, and they would have their home. We would be equals and each have the freedom to follow our separate notions of what a home should be like. It really didn't occur to me in my mid-twenties that a day might come when my parents and I would once again be sharing our home—either theirs or mine—so I didn't spend much time thinking about how we might relate to each other if we did, once again, live under the same roof.

Now my parents live in my home. Things have changed, but have they gotten easier? Relating as an adult to your parents may prove more challenging than you had ever expected; at least it has for me. In order to prepare yourself for some of the changes that will arise, it may be a good idea to review your life and the lives of your parents. My parents and I seemed to get along fine until they moved in. Then at times we would clash so strongly the jolt could be felt a block away. At first I couldn't understand what was happening. I had to slow myself down and start to examine why I was running into trouble both with my attitude and that of my parents. It helped me to stop and try to get a clear picture of the personalities involved.

One summer when I was in high school, I worked in a factory. I seemed to be the only summer girl in my department. The other young girls I worked with were slightly older and many of them had dropped out of school. They were permanent, full-time employees. Several of them invited me to go bowling with them. I thought it sounded like a great idea. My mother didn't think so. She didn't know these girls, had never met them, and did not trust them. Actually, she didn't trust anyone. She also didn't think I had enough sense to pick my friends wisely. We did battle and she won. I didn't go.

But this was the past. I was a child then. By the time my mother came to live with us, I was trying to decide whether to stay 39 for the rest of my life, or recognize 40 as a possibility. I had grown children of my own. The things of the past were just that—things of the past—or so I thought.

After much thinking, I found I had sugar-coated my memories of my mother and my childhood. My mother and I often fought back then. I was probably more defiant than my siblings and more rebellious. I wanted things my way when I was growing up, and there was no way my mother was going to bend to my will—and neither one of us had changed much over the years. We are very much alike, my mother and I. When she moved in, in some ways we simply rejoined the old battle.

Since I have a tendency to make lists and write myself questions when I'm trying to figure anything out, this is what I did to help myself get a better idea of why my mother and I seemed to be clashing and experiencing difficulty in getting along with each other. The questions I used may be helpful for you, too. Use the list before you decide to make the move. It never hurts to take a good look at yourself and those around you when making major life changes.

Who Are the Players and What Are They Like?

Who made the rules in your household when you were young?

How strict were those rules?

How did your parents react to any defiance of the rules?

What kind of punishment was meted out?

Does one of your parents have a more forceful personality than the other?

If you have brothers and sisters, who in the house most often clashed with your parents?

How did you handle your parents' rules and discipline?

Did your parents present a united front in terms of the children, or did one take all the responsibility for rule-making and discipline?

Did your family use family meetings as a method of setting family policy?

How did you react as a child to being told what to do?

How do you react to being told what to do as an adult?

Do you run your household in much the same way as your parents did theirs?

Are you a strict disciplinarian?

Do you expect family members to do what they're told without question?

Which of your parents are you most like?

What temperament does that parent have?

Think about yourself for a while. Have you developed any quirks over the years that seem to be getting more pronounced? Do you find yourself more inclined to insist not only that specific things be done around the house, but also that they be done in a specific manner? Do you find yourself becoming more like one of your parents as you grow older?

These are just simple questions to help refresh your memories of how you and your parents related to each other in your youth. Although both you and your parents have probably done a lot of changing over the years, some of the old behaviors and attitudes may resurface when your parents move in with you. Being aware of this may help prevent confusion and misunderstandings.

If you, your partner, and both of your parents are extremely easygoing and adaptable to change, you will probably have few personality problems to deal with in your new living arrangements.

Our relationship is good. I love and respect my father. I wouldn't hesitate to ask his opinion on tough decisions. I think he is very proud of me, proud of the fact that I do all the things I do and have a reasonably good job. I would say the relationship is one of mutual respect. I don't boss him around and he doesn't boss me around. He is very eager to please me and I'm eager to please him, too. He is my father so I'll always be his child, but he treats me like the mature, responsible adult that I am. (K.H.)

If, however, any one of your family members has distinct likes or dislikes that differ from your parents', you may find yourself in trouble from time to time—as Kathy goes on to point out:

I would say the relationship between my husband and my father is distant. I don't think they have a lot in common. They talk sports primarily. Although they're under the same roof, their paths don't cross a lot. They are sometimes cordial sometimes not. In some areas, they respect each other. In some areas not. (K.H.)

Before your parents move in, spend time thinking about their personalities when you were young and how they changed over the years. Sometimes the changes are not in them but in how we see them. Do they appear more mellow now, or do they seem to be becoming more entrenched in certain habits or patterns? If your parents had habitual methods of dealing with day-to-day living when you were young, these habits will probably still be in place to some degree.

My mother had developed a pattern of faking illness to avoid unpleasant chores or routine housework. She did this even when I was a small child. At such times, my older sisters would usually take care of things. Once the task was accomplished, my mother's health was quickly restored and she would grab her bowling ball and bingo chips and bolt out the front door. After my father's death, this pattern escalated and began to include frequent trips to the hospital. (P.M.)

Think also about how you interacted with them as a child and how your relationship changed as you grew. Were you allowed more freedom easily, or did you have to fight for it? Did you and your parents spend little or much time arguing about your rights and privileges? Did they accept and embrace the changes in you as you matured, or did they fight each new phase?

Karen always remembered her mother as loving, but very timid. She only has one or two memories of her mother standing up to her father. As children, she and her brothers and sisters had strict rules to follow, most of which had to do with being home most of the time and being "good" children. Although she didn't realize it until her mother moved in with her, they were taught always to put on the appearance of a happy, loving family. This was their job as children. Until Karen's mother moved in with her, Karen only remembered that her mother rarely fought. After again living with her for a while, Karen began to see a pattern of passive control that had been there all along. When Karen's mother started exerting this control on Karen's family, it caused problems that were not anticipated. Neither Karen nor her mother understood why this pattern of behavior was present.

My mother never asked for anything (when she lived with us). Even as a child I don't remember her ever asking for anything. She said she didn't want to be in the way. But somehow, and I didn't catch on for a long time, she always managed to get her way. She'd get her way, but she never asked, so no one could ever accuse her of being demanding. It was very frustrating. I knew I was being manipulated, but I wasn't sure how. My husband would get furious because I'd jump if my mother so much as sighed. Somehow, she always managed to get me to offer to do for her what she wanted.

Then I remembered that as children, it was the same way. She'd want one of us to do something, like the dusting, but she wouldn't tell us to do it. She'd tell us how hard she worked and that it was all for us and that when she was a girl, she'd always be looking for ways to help her mother. I had completely forgotten about all this until she moved in with us. Then I had trouble understanding what was happening. I'd get so angry. And Ma would just be there, placid and uncomplaining. (K.V.)

It wasn't until after Karen began attending a support group for the families of alcoholics that she began to understand her mother's behavior and feel less threatened by it. Here is how another interviewee reacted to her mother's efforts to manipulate:

Ma was a controller. She wanted to be in control. We had problems with her wanting to control me from the time I was 13. But she was never able to. That didn't stop her from trying, though. By the time she was living with us, I had mellowed and didn't resent it as much. I would just let her talk and she'd try to manipulate me and the kids. You kind of get to ignore it. (V.T.)

Keeping things such as these in mind as you strive to form a new family group will help you to anticipate possible problems. Everyone involved in your family—you, your parents, your spouse, and your children—will most likely be doing their level best to make your newly formed family a happy place to be. Everyone, however, will be entering this new situation with his or her own ideas, perceptions, problems, and background. If anyone involved, including yourself, exhibits puzzling attitudes or behavior, start by assuming there is a logical reason for the attitude or behavior. This reason may be hidden to you, and in some cases, the person himself or herself may not be aware that there is a problem. When Jane's mother started to need more and more help in remembering to do little things, Jane assumed her mother was looking for attention. This is not the way Jane's mother had lived her life and the change confused and angered Jane. Jane's mother, though, was just as confused. They began to have difficulty getting along until they found out the reason for the behavior change—Alzheimer's disease. Once the reason was known, the tension was relieved. Both women learned to cope as best they could as the disease progressed.

Problems From the Past

It is a fact of life that at times children do not get along with their parents and vice versa. Parents often have a hard time accepting decisions of the maturing children. Think about times in the past during which you and your parents clashed on matters important to each of you. Some of these might include: choice of school, or whether or not to continue school; decisions to move from your parents' home to an apartment; or the real biggie—choice of a partner or spouse. You may or may not have had any difficulties in these areas, but many people do clash with their parents over these issues.

If you had any major clashes in the past, look honestly at the overall effect they have had on your relationship with your parents. Was your relationship changed permanently? Did they lose trust in you, or you in them? Did you resent their reaction? Did they resent your defiance? Are you able to put these differences in the past and leave them there? Will these be points of tension if they live in your home?

Obviously, the most stressful point of tension would revolve around disapproval of your spouse or partner. Did they initially approve of him or her? If not, have they come to like and respect him or her? If your answer is "no" to these questions, you might want to seriously reconsider the idea of moving your parent or parents into your home.

My parents had a problem with trust. They basically didn't trust anyone. My mother said she trusted me to take care of her, but she really didn't. No one could possibly know more than she did about what was good for her. I was, however, the only person in our house that she came to almost trust. She did not believe that my husband could possibly have her welfare in mind (or mine for that matter). This lack of trust did cause severe problems. When I helped her, she would double-check everything I did and wouldn't let anyone else in the house help her at all.

She didn't think I should have married my husband to begin with. Over the years, their relationship actually became very good, but when she became really sick, all of the old attitudes came rushing back. Since she wouldn't, at first, accept anyone's help but mine, I became fairly over-whelmed. This just solidified in her mind that she had been right all along; my husband didn't have my welfare in mind —just look how run-down I was getting.

As time passed, her worsening condition made it impossible for one person to care for her, and she did learn to trust my husband to a point. It was, though, hard on everyone until this happened. Here is a similar situation:

> My mother saw my father in all men. She saw my father as the cause of all of her problems. My husband is very involved with his family—me and the children as well as his brother and sisters—but my mother, because of her life with my father, couldn't see any of this. She saw only his "weaknesses." All men are "just like your father" and therefore not to be trusted. I never knew she felt this way until she moved in with us. She always talked about how nice my husband and my brother-in-law were until she was in the same house with us. Then the hate started to come out. (K.V.)

Divided Loyalties

As people in general, and especially as parents, we have a tendency to focus most of our attention on whomever around us is most needy. If we have children and one of them is sick, we do whatever needs to be done to help that child get well. We stay up nights, administer medicine, and take the child to whatever specialists may be needed (usually regardless of the cost). In short, all else takes a back seat until that child is on the mend. The other children in the house expect this. They have probably been the center of your attention in the past. You and your spouse have a vested interest in the sick child and his or her welfare. You love that child and would probably give your life for the child.

When your parent(s) move in, you may react the same way to them. If one or the other becomes sick, you will have a tendency to focus all your attention on getting him or her better.

There is a major difference, however, that can cause problems. Your children and your partner will probably not feel exactly the same way you do about your parents. If the sickness of your parents begins to seriously disrupt your home and your ability to carry on a fairly normal family life, you may run into trouble.

> My husband became disgusted with all the emergency trips to the hospital. But he had the same problem I did—you couldn't tell when she was seriously sick and when she wasn't. You couldn't take the chance. He didn't like all the emergency trips, but at least he understood. (V.T.)

Resentment
As the child of the people who move into your home, you may get discouraged if you begin to notice resentment growing in your home over the attention your parent(s) require. Like any new arrangement, the novelty of having a grandma or grandpa living with you will wear off and daily routine will set in. You may find yourself feeling like a rubber band being stretched between the needs of your family and the needs of your parents. Quite often, when daily routine does set back in, family members expect it to be just like it was before the grandparents moved in. This probably isn't possible simply because you will have more people to deal with. Sickness, appointments, and simple daily routine tasks involving your parents will probably cut into some of the time you previously spent on yourself or on your children or

partner. Patience and understanding are going to be needed on everyone's part to keep these new demands on time from becoming problems that can cause resentments.

As my mother's health failed, she spent more and more time in the hospital. My husband would get angry at my going every day to visit her. He felt she was somewhere she was being taken care of, so I needn't be there every day. He also knew it put a strain on me—my time and my energy, not to mention my emotional state. He worried about me, not my mother. But the result was that he resented my going and spending so much time.

I resented his lack of understanding of my point of view. There was considerable tension. I tried to tell him that I went to the hospital every day as much for me as for her. I knew there wasn't much time left and would have felt terrible if something happened to her when I wasn't there. I also don't have as much faith in hospitals as he does.

Your Partner's Parent

If it is your partner's parent who has moved in and you feel your workload is increased because of it, you may begin to resent the added work. This is not abnormal. You have no childhood memories of these people. You were never cuddled or comforted by them when you were hurt or sick. You met them as adults. They are people you grew to know, and perhaps love, through your love for your partner. But there is no getting around the fact that you probably don't feel you owe them anything.

How, then, can you learn to appreciate the presence of an adult in your own home that may be a disruption to life as you knew it—a disruption like the following:

At times, my mother would seem to go to great lengths to create strife between me and my wife and our children. For example, my mother would frequently try to devalue my wife by attributing any material success we enjoyed solely to me. This was, of course, ridiculous. My wife and I worked equally hard to achieve what we had. I told her

11

this, it made no difference. The children told my mother that I was not the only contributor to the family's welfare.

Fortunately we had been forewarned by my sisters that this had been a pattern my mother had developed. Having been forewarned, my wife and I were able to deal with these disruptions. However, I still felt irritated at times that my mother would do this to the people in her life most interested in her welfare. (P.M.)

The only answer my husband and I could find for dealing with resentments over time and effort spent on our parents was to remember who they were and what they meant to the most important person in our lives. This made it much easier to take the time and to have the patience needed to try to understand what was going on with our parents rather than just getting angry or resentful if things didn't seem to be going well. It also helped us to take the time and effort to get to know each other's parents as people instead of as parents. When my husband's mother moved in with us, I expected her to be like my own mother. This was unfair. It took some time to get over my confusion and stop looking at her as a "mother" and start looking at her as a person with her own background and problems.

In Karen's case, both she and her husband became so confused about her mother's effect on the family, they decided to go to Al-Anon. This is a wonderful organization for the families of alcoholics. Although Karen's mother was not alcoholic, she had been severely damaged by her life with an alcoholic. Involvement with this group helped Karen and her husband to begin to understand the insecurities her mother must have lived with and how those insecurities affected her relationship with them.

She had a terror of being abandoned. Since my father hadn't physically abandoned her, I didn't really understand this. He had, in fact, abandoned her in his own way. He was there physically, but emotionally and spiritually he was gone. He was never there emotionally for her. Every crisis was met by his getting drunk. That would leave her to cope not only with the crisis, but also with his drinking. It would have been far kinder of him to have left her physically.

Since resentment can be a major problem to an alcoholic, much time is spent in AA meetings and in Al-Anon on the subject of resentments and how to handle them constructively. The Steps of these programs are designed to help people cope with hard times and address problems before they have a chance to turn into resentments. I learned to confront my mother when she was acting in a manipulative way instead of just stewing about things. I used the Twelve Steps of Alcoholics Anonymous to keep my own emotional state under control. It also helped that I was continually reminded by the people in the program that I couldn't change my mother. The only thing I could change was my own reaction to my mother. (K.V.)

No matter how easy going we are, combining households with our parents is bound to disrupt our lives in some way. It will take time and patience on the part of everyone involved to learn each other's habits and attitudes. Few problems, however, are impossible to solve as long as we keep open minds and when tough situations arise, give each other the benefit of the doubt.

Review

Review all of the personalities that will be involved.

Consider how you have changed over the years.

Consider realistically how you and your parents related to each other when you were a child and how you relate now.

If your parents had set ways of dealing with life when you were young, don't assume they have changed these ways.

Seriously consider how any clashes from the past affect your relationship now.

Assume that everyone involved is trying their best to adapt. If problems arise, try to find logical causes for them.

If your parents disapprove of or dislike your spouse or partner, consider finding solutions other than moving them into your home.

Deal with irritations as they arise so they don't turn into resentments.

Try to see everyone's point of view when dealing with hurt feelings caused by new distributions of time among family members.

If your birth family was for some reason dysfunctional due to such things as alcoholism, be realistic in your evaluations and get support for yourself.

2
BECOMING A CAREGIVER

If your parent becomes frail or mentally diminished as he or she grows older, you may find yourself in the position of both caring for the parent physically and making decisions with or for him or her. This can, at times, be very stressful since it is not a role we are used to playing in our parents' lives.

As in Jane's case, the lessening of faculties may be slow and at first almost imperceptible. In other cases, for example some stroke cases, the changes may be very sudden and physical disabilities may also be evident. In either case, the people interviewed and I found that, at times, we would experience great sadness. This sadness was not caused by an increased work load or fear of sickness. It seemed to be a reaction to the realization that a once-vital loved one could no longer cope with daily life, and needed help and guidance doing things both we and they once took completely for granted.

Grandma McGurn
A good example in our family of the gradually changing role from child of our parent to caregiver for our parent

occurred when my husband's mother moved in with our family.

Grandma McGurn had led a hard life. Not a life of plenty, not a particularly happy life. She was from the farms of Pennsylvania and had experienced the tragedy of her sister's death in a fire when she was young. She left the farm as a young woman and although no one seems quite sure, it is believed that she spent some time traveling with a carnival. She eventually married a man from Canada who, according to family rumor, also traveled with a carnival. Since Grandpa McGurn died long before my husband and I married, I know almost nothing about him. As it turned out, none of us—including her own children—really knew that much about Louise McGurn.

When she came to us, Louise was in her late seventies and had been living in her own apartment. She was very lonely and depressed, even though her children, one daughter especially, visited her often. My husband, with my full agreement and encouragement, asked her to live with us. She agreed. We had a spare bedroom and her things fit in nicely. She had her own television, but she also had the freedom of the house and was encouraged to be a part of the family.

Grandma McGurn seemed fairly healthy physically. However, like Virginia's mother, Grandma McGurn had, over the years, developed a problem with prescription drugs. She was not aware of this, nor were we. This is a very real physical problem faced by many elderly people. Since many elderly people do have various physical problems, they sometimes go to several different specialists. Sometimes these specialists know of the patients' other doctors and the medications those doctors have prescribed, but sometimes they don't. If not monitored carefully, the prescriptions can increase in number and become a real danger to the elderly person. When this situation occurs, it is almost always out of ignorance rather than neglect. The elderly patient may not think to tell his or her eye doctor about a drug he or she is taking or the medications that a cardiologist has prescribed. The elderly patient may not be aware of the interaction of different drugs and how harmful they can be. This is what happened in Grandma McGurn's case. She had moved several times and would go to a new doctor in her new neighborhood. The doctor would prescribe for whatever specific problem Grandma was there for, but Grandma almost never thought to tell the doctor that she had other prescriptions. The result for Grandma McGurn, and for many elderly people like her, was a mix of problems that were very hard to diagnose and treat. The symptoms she had would change depending on what medication she was taking at any given time. At the time Grandma lived with us, no one had a clue about prescription drug problems. All we knew was that Grandma acted very strangely at times.

Grandma Sleeps with Her Eyes Open

At first, Grandma seemed to be adjusting fairly well. She would sit with us in the living room in the evening and watch television. Although she did not cook at this point, we enjoyed family dinners, and except for bananas (which she said gave her convulsions), her dietary needs were not unusual. During the day, everything seemed fairly normal. We went about our usual business.

It was in the evening and especially late at night that we started having problems. The first sign that Grandma was going to be a bit different was her insistence on sitting between me and my husband on the couch when we watched TV. There were plenty of other places to sit, but she insisted on sitting smack between us. I found this uncomfortable, and so did my husband. At first we felt it would pass as she became more comfortable and secure in her new home. Not so. Instead of letting up, it got worse. If we stayed up until three in the morning, so did she. She would fall asleep on the couch, but she wouldn't budge from it until we went to bed. This may seem like a little thing, but Grandma slept with her eyes open and rolled up in her head. To have someone sound asleep in your living room with her eyes wide open and rolled up in her head can be very disconcerting. I started to fear that she would die on that couch and I wouldn't know the difference. How would I explain to the police that she had been dead for four hours in my living room, and I never noticed?

When my husband went on the midnight shift, Grandma's insecurities seemed to escalate. Grandma would come into my room and wake me sometime between 3:00 and 4:00 every morning to tell me that she was dying. At first, I believed her. If my own mother said she was dying, she probably was. After a while, though, it became apparent that she just couldn't sleep and wanted company. Although I could understand this need, I was getting run-down and irritable due to lack of sleep. She did not do this when her son was in the house, only when he worked through the night.

At this point, one of my more logical children suggested that I lock my bedroom door. What an idea! It simply hadn't occurred to me to lock my door. The night I locked my door, Grandma found the kids' "secret passage." Ours was the front bedroom in the house. Our closet doubled as the guest closet. There were two entrances to the closet. One in the front hallway and another in the bedroom. You could enter the bedroom through the closet from the front hallway. When we moved into the house, the kids loved it. They would sneak into our room in hopes of scaring us. Often, they did. For them, it was much more fun than coming through the regular bedroom door. It was the passage the puppy used if the other door was closed since I rarely close a closet door securely. Often we would hear the puppy tripping over shoes to get into our room when she woke in the night and wanted company.

For some reason that I didn't understand for some time, I found this sneaking into our room cute on the part of the kids and the puppy, but completely unsettling on the part of Grandma McGurn. To my half-asleep brain, noise in the closet meant a long-eared basset puppy overcoming hurdles that would eventually put her where she wanted to be—in a nice warm bed. It definitely did not mean a near-80-year-old, skeletal lady with disheveled white hair and sunken eyes. Grandma successfully took 20 years off my life the night she came through the closet, and broke me of locking my bedroom door. If I had to be awakened, it was easier to cope with if she came through the bedroom door than through the bedroom closet. Actually, her motives for coming into the bedroom—through the door or closet—were the same as the puppy's—she wanted to feel warm and safe. She was afraid to be alone.

We talked about this, both between ourselves and with Grandma. My husband asked her to stop waking the house every night. She agreed, but come the next night, the same thing would happen. We all got frustrated. As the frustration grew, so did the problems. Grandma started accusing the children of petty thefts—quarters and dimes—from her dresser. They all had part-time jobs and had no need of her money. Their usual answer to her accusations was, "Here, Grandma, do you need some money? I have some, take this." And they would hand her several dollar bills.

Grandma also made frequent emergency trips to the hospital. She would think she was having a heart attack and want us to call an ambulance. This we always did. She was not, however, having heart attacks. She was having reactions to the medications she was taking. Although Grandma could not help her behavior, it was disruptive to the family as a whole. She not only confused herself, she confused us, and she confused the doctors. Unfortunately for all of us, very little was known at the time about prescription drug problems and the elderly.

Grandma McGurn eventually went into a nursing home. However, before that happened, she gradually lost the ability to make rational decisions and to take care of her daily needs. She would forget to eat if she was not reminded. She would wear the same apron day after day unless someone took it away forcing her to put on a clean one. Because her stomach always bothered her, she would give herself enemas until she became dehydrated. When we refused to buy the enemas, she would send the kids to the store to get them. We eventually had to have the kids report any shopping requests from Grandma to us. Left to herself, she was dangerous to her own health.

The Child as Caregiver

This is probably one of the hardest things for a child—no matter what age the child is—to go through: a parent's growing neediness. Grandma McGurn had reached a point where she could no longer function independently. She needed increasing amounts of attention. She was not senile. She was, however, ill.

> My mother was not a bad person. She was a sick person. I realized that because of her illness, her judgment had been affected and that I would now have to set limits on her behavior. (P.M.)

It is very hard for a child to become a caregiver to a parent. This is, after all, the person who had taken care of them, fulfilled their needs, been strong and protective. To take over the role as caregiver to your own parent feels very much like giving up on them. It is, in fact, admitting their mortality. If you love your parents, the realization that they are no longer the people they used to be and that they probably only have a short time left with you can be crushing.

We feel comfortable with our children when they want to snuggle and sit on our laps, or like Grandma McGurn did, sit between us on a couch. We understand the needs of a child for touching and love. It makes us feel good that our children look to us for warmth and comfort. We can even understand the need of a puppy to break house rules and climb on the bed or couch to snuggle with the people it needs to trust and love. It is very hard for us, though, to understand the sometimes overwhelming needs of the elderly for these same things.

She's very afraid. She's afraid something is going to happen to her and someone is not going to be right there with her. This is something you're never going to change about her. She has these little attacks and the first thing out of her mouth is "Don't leave me." The kids could be tearing up the back of the house and she'll still say, "Don't leave me." I have to be right there next to her even though there is little I can do. (S.L.)

When my mother first started having problems, I would become terribly angry with her. I thought she was acting helpless on purpose. After all, she had always taken care of her own financial affairs and taken care of the house. When she suddenly seemed incapable of doing simple things like finding her shoes or remembering to bathe, I became confused and angry. I thought she just decided that she wanted me to wait on her. I was wrong. She was exhibiting the first signs of Alzheimer's disease. (J.M.)

The Space Theory
We have been taught that people need their "space." We try not to cross the invisible barriers that define other people's space. Many studies have been done on this subject. Books have been written both on how not to violate other's space and how to violate it to get what we want.

Children have no respect for the "space" theory. When they want to be close, they get close. We know this, we understand this, and usually we enjoy this. We expect adults to respect our space and stay their distance. Adults, however, often yearn for the closeness that children demand.

In our early and middle adulthood, we usually control this yearning and tell ourselves it is childish to need this kind of closeness. Often, the elderly, especially the physically or emotionally needy elderly, once again demand the closeness they need. Unfortunately this often puts the other adults around them in direct conflict with the ideas of space they have come to understand. It is sometimes very hard for adult children to respond to the need of their parents for touching and hugging. We often misunderstand when our parents do reach out to us for the attention they need.

My wife had purchased a machine that tests blood-sugar level in order to monitor her father's levels—he is diabetic. The test was fairly simple. My wife's mother began to show what seemed like resentment at the attention being shown by my wife to her father. My mother-in-law began to demand breakfast at the same time my wife would be testing her father's blood sugar.

On one occasion, my wife began the test at which time her mother came to the kitchen table and said she wanted soft-boiled eggs. My wife replied that she would be finished with the test in a minute and would then cook the eggs. At this, my mother-in-law actually banged her spoon on the table and shouted, "I want my eggs now."

Our eldest son happened to be passing through the kitchen at the time and witnessed this outburst. He stopped in his tracks and stared in disbelief at his grand-mother, just as I did. At this point, I think my wife's mother suddenly became fully conscious of her conduct and became visibly embarrassed. What struck me at the time as so incredible was that both my wife's parents were mature, responsible, well-informed, well-intentioned adults, but sometimes they would seem to snap and act in fairly bizarre ways. Perhaps their various health problems sometimes caused them to need more than we could give. Their behavior sometimes seemed very erratic. We didn't know how to respond. (P.M.)

This type of behavior is, of course, totally unacceptable. All people, young and old, need feedback on their behavior. If a parent is mentally alert, he or she needs to be told when his or her behavior is unacceptable. It is also helpful to try to understand why our parents may now demand attention they didn't seem to need before.

It helps here to think back to our own childhood, and if we have children, to their childhoods. When were we, or our children, most in need of contact and comfort? For most people the answer would probably be when we were sick or hurt and in the deep of the night when the monsters in the closet and under the bed woke us with nightmares. The loving concern of our parents made us feel safe, made us feel less sick, made us feel that all would be well again.

When are our elderly parents most in need of contact and comfort? When they are sick or hurt or afraid. Grandma McGurn didn't sleep at night because she was afraid to. My own mother rarely slept at night. In their cases, too much medication, failing health, or sleeping too much during the day made getting through the night very difficult.

My Mother

In the last few months of my mother's life, she often woke me in the night. There was always a reason. Did I fix her medicine for the morning? She had dropped something she desperately needed. She hit the intercom button by mistake. The cat was in her room. She thought there was something wrong with the oxygen machine. She couldn't find her flashlight (which she used to lure the cat into her room). She did, in fact, always have a good underlying reason for waking me —she was afraid. She was afraid she would have trouble breathing. She was afraid the intercom wasn't working. She was afraid that if she didn't watch the night, she wouldn't see the next day. Since it wasn't part of my mother's makeup to be afraid and dependent, she was ashamed to just say she was afraid.

Sometimes, on these nightly watches, I would remember times I had stayed up with my children when they were sick. I don't remember getting mad at them. I remember one particularly stormy night when the kids, whose bedrooms were upstairs closer to the storm, woke me in the middle of the night because they were afraid. I didn't get angry at them.

I also remembered my own childhood. I was given to nightmares and often woke up screaming. My mother would come to me and get me back to sleep. I don't remember her getting angry at me. Why, then, did I often find myself getting angry with my mother for waking me in the middle of the night? I'm not sure, but I've come to believe that the anger was not because she was waking me. The anger was a result of fear—hers and mine. She had always been strong. I never really remember her showing fear when we were kids. She was scaring me to death because she was afraid. I often react to my own fear by getting angry at the thing that is scaring me. She was scaring me. When my children were small, their waking me didn't scare me. They were afraid of the usual things kids are afraid of. They were really very healthy, so sitting up with them when they were sick was a matter of comfort, not one of impending loss. With my mother it was different. I never knew when the buzzer went off if I would find her in a truly critical state or if she just wanted something. I usually expected the worst. I didn't want her to die. It's amazing how many crises I could imagine in the trip down the stairs to her room.

They Aren't Children

The big difference, then, in tending to your parents is that they may seem to demand some of the types of things that children do, but they are not children. They are adults caught in a strange tug-of-war between wanting and needing nurturing, and their desire to be healthy, productive people.

In my mother's case, we were desperately trying to get her on her feet. We were afraid that if she didn't start moving around, she would develop pneumonia. She did, in fact, do just that. One of her doctors took a hard line and insisted that she was physically able, and she was. It is easy to forget, though, that our physical bodies are only a part of us. Her physical body may have been strong enough, but she could not control the fear. She was terrified of not being able to breathe. So terrified, in fact, that she was never able to get up again after her last hospitalization.

Eight and Eighty Cannot Be Compared

We see so many "success" stories on TV and at the movies about people who overcome physical disability and go on with their lives. Young men and women who have terrible accidents and walk again, or at least accomplish great things despite their disabilities or injuries. Often in these accounts we are shown times during which they give up and someone forces them, using a tough line, to get up and try again.

The key word in that description is "young." When dealing with our parents, we are not dealing with young people who have all of the resources of youth at their disposal. We are dealing with people who have probably picked themselves up a million times. People who have fought discouragement and fear over and over in their lives. People who probably put on a brave front for us thousands of times. Now, though, if they are sick or diminished in any way, they are looking their own mortality square in the eye and they need help. Sometimes, especially in the frail elderly, it just isn't possible for them to be brave anymore. They are afraid and desperately need comfort more than encouragement.

No matter how strong a person's faith is, passing on to the next world is something they've never done before, and it can be a frightening thought to them. It's easy to expound about not fearing death when you're young and strong and death is just a hazy idea relegated to the far distant future. It takes on a completely different aspect if you are old and sick and have little hope of getting any better or stronger.

My mother couldn't be left alone. She was afraid to be alone. She would try to find us if she couldn't see us. We always had to have someone in the house with her. Once, before we realized how badly the Alzheimer's disease had affected her, she went looking for us. We weren't there so she left the house to look for us and couldn't get back in.

25

She broke a window trying to get in and cut herself. One of the neighbor's sons saw her and took her to his house. They fixed her arm and stayed with her until we got home. We never left her alone again. (J.M.)

Listen to Your Own Instincts

With my own mother, I did something I will probably regret for the rest of my life. I wanted desperately for her to stay with us and be as happy as possible. I listened to the doctor instead of listening to my instincts. I let him convince me that a hard line was the way to go in getting my mother up again. He was wrong, but he didn't really know her. He didn't understand her as a person. I was wrong because I did know her. I knew that this wasn't the solution and that if there was any way she could have gotten up again she would have, but I was grasping at straws. Each day that went by, I became more desperate to get her out of bed and moving around. Each day the struggle got harder for both of us. She knew what I was trying to do, she understood. She just wasn't capable of overcoming her fears and getting up again.

At one point during this time, my mother became especially frustrated and told me I should forget the other people in the family and just take care of her. This would make her happy. It was, of course, impossible. She knew it. I knew it. But she had in the past done it for me. When I was young, I contracted whooping cough. She left the rest of the family to tend to itself and took care of me. She centered all of her energy on getting me well again. It worked. I got well.

She knew she was dying and simply wanted and needed the care and attention she had given me. She was sick and afraid and in need of a mother's care. I was overwhelmed. I knew that if I did what she asked, I would eventually alienate my husband and children. Worst of all, it wouldn't work. She just wasn't going to get better. As much as she needed me, I needed my husband and children. I was just as frightened by what was going on as she was. I needed her. She, even in my adult years, was someone I could go to for comfort. She was on my side. I didn't want to lose her. I couldn't stop what was happening and I became angry at her, at the situation, and especially at her need to be taken care of.

My mother eventually needed someone to do everything for her. She needed someone to bathe her, to feed her, and to change her. She became very frail and would fall and hurt herself if she tried to walk alone. I admit, at first, I was very angry at her. I felt betrayed. No matter what I did, it didn't work. She just kept getting worse and worse. (J.M.)

The Worst of Times

Often, our parents' needs for attention come at the worst possible times for us. We can become overtired and resentful if we are not getting enough rest or enough time just to be with ourselves doing things for ourselves. It is very difficult at such times to remain patient and understanding.

She would always get sick around dinner time. I used to ask her, "Can't you ever get sick during the day instead of at dinner time when I'm busy?" I had to pick my husband up and make dinner for all the kids and that was when she wanted to go to the hospital. She said, "Those people (my husband and kids) can take care of themselves. They're not the ones who are sick. I'm sick. I need you. They don't." I felt she was competing for my time and attention. It was like when my kids were little. They would compete for my time and attention, but they were just babies then. They competed with each other. Then when Ma seemed to start doing the same thing, I had a hard time with it. She couldn't stand it that I had to pay attention to the kids. I found this hard to deal with. It made me angry. Everyone was willing to have her fit in with the family, but she didn't seem to want to fit in. She seemed to want to be the center of attention. (V.T.)

What to do? How can we balance our time and emotions under these circumstances? With other members of our family, we don't give in to every demand for time and attention. We do a mental ranking of needs and wants and choose the demands we can agree to meet and those we cannot.

Sometimes we can take our kids to the park when they want to go and sometimes we can't. There are times we interrupt our workday for doctor's appointments and other times we arrange the appointments around our work schedules. We may have a general housekeeping schedule but sometimes we let the housekeeping go to fit in a necessary appointment or just to indulge in a fun activity; sometimes we don't. We juggle our time every day whether our parents live with us or not. If our parents move in with us, we may be faced with more juggling, but our normal needs and wants ranking will usually still work. If doctor's appointments are necessary, discuss your schedule with the doctors so the appointments can be made at the most convenient time for the person who will be taking the parent to the doctor. If your parents have old friends they want to socialize with, find times when they can invite friends over and have some privacy. If your parents can no longer drive, find out which of their friends can drive and if it would be convenient for them to pick your parents up from time to time.

On the other hand, if your parent wants something at a time that is inconvenient for you, tell them that it just isn't a good time. We sometimes forget that our parents, too, spent many hours juggling schedules and are probably more aware than we think of how busy we really are. Keep in mind, though, that like you, your parents aren't mind readers. They can't possibly know when you are or are not busy. Let them know what is convenient for you and what is not.

My mother finally reached the point where I felt I could no longer take care of her. It was very, very sad. I had had my first child and there were some medical problems with him that called for weekly doctor visits on the other side of the city. We didn't have a car at the time, so I had to take the bus. I also had to make sure someone was with Ma while I was away. My sisters and I finally decided to look into a nursing home—something we never imagined having to do—but then Ma had a stroke. She never came home again after that. (J.M.)

My own mother's physical and emotional conditions deteriorated. Eventually, the medication she needed in order to breathe destroyed her stomach lining and she died of peritonitis caused by a perforated ulcer. Everyone involved had done everything possible for her. Her body gave out from a 15-year battle with illness.

In Grandma McGurn's case, although her physical condition remained good, her emotional condition deteriorated. There was much we did not know about her emotional condition that we have pieced together since she passed away. As I have said previously, she had become addicted to several of the medications she was taking. We, me and her own children, were not aware of this. We did know she had a remarkable number of prescriptions. We also realized she could effectively fake almost any illness she wanted to. She was good at getting herself admitted to hospitals. However, since this all took place many years ago, and none of us were in the medical profession or had experiences with professional counselors, it never occurred to us to try to get her help for her addictions. She definitely didn't fit anyone's idea of an addicted person. She was in her seventies and was only taking prescription drugs.

Hers was a problem that many elderly people do have. Today, people in general, and people in the medical profession are much more aware of the problems the elderly face with medications. Both the dosages and the interplay of different prescription drugs are subjects in need of extensive study. As caregivers for our parents, we may find ourselves in a position where we feel there is a problem with our parents' medications. These concerns should be brought immediately to the attention of the doctor. We need also to be sure that each specialist our parent consults is fully aware of every other doctor involved in our parent's care and every medication our parent is taking. Since many frail elderly people do have memory problems, supervision of medications can become one of our most important caregiving tasks.

Eventually, we had to place Grandma McGurn in a nursing home. This was hard on everyone, but her problems were disrupting our home to the point of insanity. We failed to see her sickness for what it was—a true illness. The bright spot, however, was that she seemed to prefer a hospital-like atmosphere to living in a home where attentions are divided. She did come to be content in the nursing home before she passed away. She seemed more secure there.

Resentments did grow over this time with Grandma McGurn because we did not understand what was happening. The children, although they coped, certainly did not like being accused of things they had not done.

Since we didn't understand her illness, in fact, we couldn't even find someone to tell us what her illness was, we mistook some of her symptoms as mean and self-centered games. I resented her apparent dislike for me and the kids resented being accused of stealing, and being treated by Grandma, at times, as annoyances. My husband was disappointed that his mother seemed unhappy when he was trying hard to make her life pleasant. He resented what appeared to be false emergencies.

We did the best we could to find out what was going on with Grandma. No one, including the doctors, seemed able to help. We did manage, however, to concentrate on the good times, and minimize the stressful times.

Know Your Family

Both my husband and I realized that, although our children had their faults, stealing from little old ladies was not among them. The children knew we were not going to trounce them when Grandma accused them of stealing. My husband, although not entirely sure what his mother's problems were, was aware the problems were with her and acted accordingly. We tried not to allow her illness to disrupt the family. When it finally did become too disruptive, he was the one who suggested we start looking for a nursing home.

His sisters were great about taking responsibility for Grandma McGurn even though she lived in our home. They visited and took her out to play bingo and other places she wanted to go. This was all very important. With the feeling that we were working as a team and as a family to deal with a family problem, no one ended up with lasting resentments. We grew closer because of the experience. We also gained a better understanding of our own coping abilities.

Burnout

Don't feel too bad if, at times, you find yourself overwhelmed with a strong desire to run away from home. You are not alone. You are not weak. You are just human. Even professionals in the field of geriatrics or in the field of terminal illness find themselves overwhelmed at times by the emotional strain of taking care of people who are probably not going to get better. Most people taking care of their parents are not professional. Here is a typical case of burnout:

> At times I would just sit down and cry. My mother was no longer the person I had known all my life. She seemed like a child, but where I could look forward to my child growing up, all I could look forward to with my mother was a worsening of her condition and her eventual death. God, it was so depressing at times. (J.M.)

Like Jane, I, too, became very depressed at times. In the cases of both of our mothers, they were dealing with fatal health conditions. We knew this. Certainly periods of depression or burnout would have been much different and probably less intense had they been basically healthy and suffering only minor problems concerned with the aging process. In all cases, however, some burnout can be expected simply because our parents are aging and are no longer capable of doing all of the things they used to be able to do. Looking to people outside your home for help and solace can dramatically reduce stress you are feeling in dealing with your parents.

Sources of Help

I looked to friends for the support I needed—friends who were willing to listen to my fears and reassure me. My husband also turned to friends for help. Although my husband and I helped each other as much as we could, neither of us could be the sole emotional support for the other. It would have been too much to ask. We were both too involved.

If you do nothing else for your own emotional stability and health, do this: Find people outside your home to talk to. Many hospitals now have support groups for people involved with taking care of their aging parents. Get involved with one of these groups. It will help. You will be talking to people who understand.

If you can't either emotionally or physically cope with talking to strangers, or you simply can't get out of the house, as was often the case with me, develop a phone network of caring friends. Don't be afraid of sounding uncaring by telling someone how frustrated or angry or frightened you sometimes feel. They will understand that you wouldn't be feeling this way unless you really cared.

People need people—you are no different. Don't cut off your support lines. The more emotional support you can get, the better able you will be to be loving and caring toward your parents, no matter how ill they become.

My husband and I found we really couldn't cope without help. We went to Al-Anon. I had been going to AA for years and that helped me get as far as I did, but I needed more. I thought, perhaps my reactions were abnormal because of my past drinking history. We went to Al-Anon at first because of me. We thought maybe my drinking had made me look at things strangely. But after a while, we began to recognize many of my mother's behaviors as co-dependent, behaviors that are apparently very common in the family members of alcoholics—passive dependency, fear of abandonment, manipulation. We were more able to cope and understand what Mom had gone through and why she was the way she was. It helped tremendously. At least we realized that we weren't losing our minds. (K.V.)

The hospital put me in contact with an Alzheimer's support group. These are all people who have had to cope with Alzheimer's disease in one way or another. I found out that the anger and hopelessness I felt were normal. Although it was very difficult for me to get out of the house, I could call the people in this group and talk about how I felt and what was going on. They understood. They had been there. They helped me go on. And they helped me to take better and more loving care of my mother. I am very grateful for their help and understanding. (J.M.)

Review

Realistically look at the state of your parent's health, both physical and emotional.

If your parent's health is failing, be prepared to become a caregiver for that parent.

Consider your own physical and emotional strength before committing to the care of a frail parent.

Keep in mind that the health of your parents will probably change over time. What is possible for them to do today may be impossible tomorrow.

Remember that your parents are not children and cannot

be treated as such.

Keep in mind that your parents' need for nurturing may increase as they become more needy.

Rank the needs and wants of your parents for your time and energy in the same way you do for the rest of the family.

If a parent's needs or wants seriously clash with your ability to fulfill them, tell your parent and ask for his or her advice.

Find help for yourself. Build a support network you can depend on.

Do not feel guilty if you at times find yourself resenting the whole situation. This is normal and will probably pass. Contact your support network at times like these.

3
LOOKING AT RESPONSIBILITY

Boy Scouts are taught to do their duty. I was never a Girl Scout, but I imagine they are also taught to do their duty. Most of us as children are taught in one way or another to do our duty. Our duty as little children may only be to tidy our rooms or walk the dog. The fact remains, though, that as children we had duties we were expected to perform and were probably punished if we failed to perform these duties and live up to our responsibilities. When we got a little older, it was our responsibility to behave and do well in school. Then it was our responsibility to grow up and get a job. Now we are faced with another question of duty and just exactly what our responsibility is. Three questions you must ask yourself before you ask your parent to move in are: What are my responsibilities toward my parents? What are my responsibilities toward my family? What are my responsibilities to myself?

The first one is a tough question. Our parents are the people who raised us. In most instances, we know that they sacrificed for us as we grew. We probably feel that we owe them much. On the other hand, there is that old comeback: "I didn't ask to be born. I had no choice in the matter." Both of these positions are true. Our parents did care for us and love us but that was the responsibility they took on when they decided to have children. They knew, or should have known, that raising children took a major commitment, and that children can't take care of themselves.

So the strictly technical answer to "What do we owe our parents?" or "What is our duty or responsibility to them?" is probably, "We owe them nothing." Our duty and responsibility is to be honest, upstanding citizens who bring honor to their name. This is, however true, a totally unsatisfactory answer for almost everyone. Most of us do feel that we owe our parents something, and that we do have a responsibility to them. Here are some typical responses to the question "What do we owe our parents?"

My duty is to take care of my mother. I hate nursing homes. I'd never, ever consider a nursing home. It (a nursing home) would have to be the absolute last resort. With my father, you couldn't contain him. He was getting violent. There was nothing that could be done. We had no choice (but to put him in a nursing home). If she was at a point where she had to have constant care, for example, if she needed a nurse, we'd hire one. If she couldn't afford it, the family would chip in. (S.L.)

I feel you have to do whatever you can for them (your parents). Whatever they need. (V.T.)

It's our duty to see that our parents' needs are met when they get older. By that I mean food, shelter, emotional support, and love. (P.M.)

I think my duty is to be supportive, loving, respectful, and caring. If he should need more of each of these things as he continues to age, my duty is to continue to assume them. If any kinds of situations manifest to the extent that more support is needed, whether it be financial or medical, whatever, my duty is to be sure that he gets the best that he needs. (K.H.)

It is important that you find out exactly how you feel on all three questions, since your feeling about them will affect how you react to your parents once they have moved in. Answering the following questions may help you as it did me.

How Do I Feel?

What do I mean by the word duty?

What do I see my duty or responsibility toward my parents as?

Why do I feel this way?

If I have brothers and sisters, what do I feel their duty or responsibility to our parents is? Why?

What do I think my parents see as my responsibility to them?

How did these ideas of duty or responsibility come about? (Did I learn them from my parents? Does society tell me this is the way I should feel?)

Do I have a balanced perception of duty in my life as a whole?

How do I think my ideas of duty or responsibility will affect my relationship with my parents?

How do I think their ideas of duty or responsibility will affect our relationship?

What does my partner feel that his or her duty or responsibility to my parents is?

What does my partner feel his or her duty or responsibility to his or her own parents is?

What does my partner feel that his or her duty or responsibility to me is?

What do I feel my duty or responsibility to my partner is?

I have come to believe that the idea of "duty" can be the single most destructive element at play where our relationship with our parents is concerned when they move in. We can become very muddled between the idea of duty and the idea of love. Love and duty and responsibility are not synonymous words. To me, duty is a word used in the context of "I really don't want to do this, but it is my duty, so I will."

Many people thought that I asked my parents to move in with us for several reasons: (1) They needed help. (This was the chief reason I had for doing it.) (2) It was my responsibility as one of their daughters. (Wrong. It was not my responsibility. It was my decision.) (3) My sister couldn't be expected to do it because her family had undergone a terrible tragedy, the death of one of their children in an automobile accident. (This was true. I never would have expected my sister to undergo the strain of taking on the care of my mother, who was very ill at the time. My sister and her family had all they could do to get on with their lives.) (4) I was the youngest and therefore had been the last to leave home. (This was given as their reason by some of the people I interviewed. I'm not really sure how this type of reasoning makes sense to anyone.) (5) My house was big enough. (This was, in fact, also one of the most important factors in the whole decision: Which one of the children had the room?)

As for myself, the "why's" of the decision came down to some very simple emotional issues. I did not feel that it was my duty. I asked my parents to move in with us because I loved them and wanted to help them. I knew my mother dreaded the thought of going to a nursing home. She saw that as being abandoned, and she had a great fear of abandonment. I simply loved her and thought she would be happier and feel more secure in our home, where there were lots of people around. My father is very hard of hearing and, at times, couldn't hear her if she called for him. This frightened her terribly. It was a simple wish to allay some of those fears that was the driving force behind our decision to move my parents into our home. Duty or responsibility had nothing to do with it. I did my "duty" to my parents by not turning out to be an ax-murderer. I showed my love by wanting them to live with the rest of the people I love, my family.

The fact that you or I do not feel it is our duty to take care of our parents does not necessarily mean that your parents feel the same way. Many parents do, in fact, feel it is the duty of their children to take care of them in their old age. If you feel you are taking your parents in out of love, but they feel you are merely doing what is expected of you, there may be problems.

You can get some idea of what your parents think about duties and responsibilities by thinking back to your childhood. How did your parents react to what you felt were special experiences or honors? If you worked hard to increase a grade in school, were you praised or were you told that you were finally performing the way you should have all along? If you tried something new, did your parents praise your effort, or did they instruct you on your areas of weakness?

Your answers to these questions may help you to prepare for your parents' attitudes when they move in. Don't expect them to change. If your parents treated your successes and accomplishments as examples of your merely doing your duty as a child, they may have the same reaction to your moving them into your homes. If you are simply doing what is expected of you, then there is no need on their parts to be overly thankful for or appreciative of your effort. If this happens, you may find it frustrating.

If, on the other hand, your parents appreciated extra effort and the willingness to try in you as a child, they will probably recognize the love and effort involved in your taking over their care.

Be as realistic in this evaluation of your childhood as you can. It will help you to understand the personality dynamics that are taking place around you when your parents do move in.

What is Your Partner's Responsibility to Your Parents?

Once again, the simple if disturbing answer is: "Your partner has no responsibility toward your parents. None at all." If your partner has agreed, and it is to be hoped readily and happily agreed, to have your parents move in, he or she should be doing it out of love—not necessarily love for them, but love for you and respect for your love of them. This does not mean that either you or your partner are going to find the living arrangements completely compatible at all times. You are not the person you were when you lived with your parents, and, in all probability, your partner never lived with your parents. Human beings have disagreements and they can find each other irritating at times. The key to general happiness in this situation is not duty, but mutual respect.

If you remember that your partner is acting out of love for you, and your partner remembers that you are acting out of love for your parents, you should be able to maintain a reasonably smooth relationship in every area. People who do things out of perceived "duty" have a tendency to end up feeling like martyrs. Martyrs are not usually very happy with their state in life and can make everyone else as unhappy as they are.

What Are Your Parents' Responsibilities Toward You and Your Family?

Assuming your parents are needy enough to have to move in with one of their children, they are probably no longer in a position to fulfill any duty—real or perceived. Their time of fulfilling duties or obligations is past. Anything they do for you or your family, other than show everyone involved respect, is a gift, and it should be a gift of love and not one given out of a sense of owing.

Guests?

Most people do become guests with respect to people who used to be simply family. We become guests in our parents' homes after we move out and become adults. They become guests in our homes when they come to visit. While visiting in our parents' home, we observe the rules of conduct set down by our parents. We know what type of conduct is acceptable or not acceptable while in their home. These rules may not be the same rules we observe in our home. For example, perhaps your parents don't smoke and you do. They may have a no-smoking rule in effect in their home. We need to respect this rule while we are in their home. Maybe your parents let their pets on the furniture and you don't allow your dog on the furniture in your home. When your parents are visiting in your home, they wouldn't consider encouraging the dog to get on the couch with them. The rules of behavior for visits are known and observed. We each acknowledge the right of the other to make the rules for our own homes.

When parents move in with their children, the dynamics change. They are no longer guests in our home. It becomes their home, too. Psychological adjustments need to be made so that everyone can and does experience the feeling of being "home." Duty rarely plays an important role in building a warm and loving home. We do things for each other because we want to, not because it is our duty to do these things. We are aware of our children's feelings and those of our partner, not because we are expected to, but because we become attuned to the moods of the people we love. We have a desire to comfort them, to protect them, and to make them feel wanted and loved.

When our parents move in with us, these very same dynamics need to be put into motion for them. We want to make them feel welcomed and loved. We want to make them feel that they are where they belong, not simply that we are doing what we are expected to do. Being a whole and complete extended family is the goal that everyone—you, your partner, your children, and your parents—should be working toward.

Your parents will probably have some income, and will most likely offer to pay for their room and board. Although I, and most of the people I talked to, at first rejected the idea of our parents paying for the privilege of living with us, most of us do now take some sort of monetary payment. In our case and several others, this takes the form of a set amount every month. In all cases, the amount mentioned was not even close to the amount it would take the parents to live on their own. In other cases, the parent involved does not give a set amount, but has chosen certain necessities of the household at large to pay for. This may be groceries, or utility bills, or repair bills. Again, the amounts of money involved do not match the amount it would take them to be totally self-supporting.

My first reaction to my mother's offer of money was to turn it down. She became adamant about giving us something for room and board. She finally said she wouldn't move in unless we accepted the money.

The reason most parents who are able to offer money do and the reason that the offer should be accepted, has to do with feeling like part of the family. At first, I was afraid my parents would feel like boarders if I took the money. It finally dawned on me that every person in the family was contributing to the welfare of the whole family in one way or another. My husband and I were working. The kids were working to pay for college. The youngest had a part-time job to pay for the extras she wanted such as her own car. Everyone also had jobs around the house they were responsible for.

My parents, and probably your parents, are accustomed to supporting themselves. They need to contribute to the house they are now living in just as much as they needed to contribute to the home they came from. The people interviewed for this book all said their parents did not consider contributing financially to the family as a duty. They simply felt it was a part of any family's life. Everyone contributes in whatever way they can.

Review

Review your ideas of duty and responsibility to yourself and to your family.

Try to get the idea of duty out of the picture. Work from a base of love and respect rather than one of responsibility.

Foster the feeling that no one is a guest and that everyone is simply a member of the family.

Allow your parents to contribute in any way they can to their new home.

4

UNDERSTANDING ANGER

I stood behind the wall and stuck my tongue out. Having already screwed up my face into a mask of rage and frustration, it made quite a picture. This was just the face I had been warned would freeze that way if I continued to make it. The object of this tantrum? My mother. There were times as a child I was sure she was the meanest, most unfair person on the face of the earth. And although she was well past the point of sticking her tongue out at me or making grotesque faces, I certainly could see the anger flare in her eyes no matter how well she was able to control her voice and actions.

Over the years, I am sure my own kids have stuck a tongue or two out at me and have seen the anger in my eyes as I fought to control my voice and reactions.

Anger is a part of life. It is even part of healthy relationships. No two human beings are alike. Each has his or her own needs and perceptions. Anger develops when a person feels that his or her needs are being ignored and treated lightly. Anger develops when one person tries to force opinions on another. Anger can develop when people become afraid for one reason or another. Anger can develop when people feel helpless in a situation. Anger can find countless reasons for being. Anger frightens people. Anger can be devastating, or it can be an agent of change for the better. It will definitely come into play when dealing with the life changes involved with bringing parents into your home.

Anger at the Situation

One of the first angers that I felt, and that you may feel is anger at the situation itself. The move of a parent into your home usually means that either you have already lost someone you loved, one of your parents, or someone you love and saw as strong and able to handle all problems has become debilitated for some reason. Certainly if one of your parents dies, leaving the other heartsick and afraid, anger is a very possible reaction. This will usually pass in time as you and your parent get on with the problems of daily living. Time does heal wounds. There is no need to be afraid of this anger at the situation. It is normal and will pass.

Anger at Your Parent

The reality that one of your parents cannot cope with a situation, either the death of the other or an illness, can also be a cause for anger. We usually have unrealistic notions of our parents' abilities to cope with the problems of this world. After all, they were the ones who solved our problems, who took care of us, and made us feel safe. To realize that they are simply human beings who have reached a point that they cannot deal with everyday problems on their own can be frightening. This fear can make us angry. Often, we become angry at them for letting us down in some unknown way, as, for example, the following reactions indicate.

My mother was in a terrible predicament. She was a hypochondriac cursed with a strong body. In order to be admitted to a hospital, she would starve herself for days and use enemas to dehydrate herself. This would make me angry. She had a nice home and was surrounded by people who loved her. It was hard to accept the idea that she would rather be sick. This need to be sick stopped her from enjoying life. Even though I knew she had severe emotional problems that she apparently couldn't control, it did make me angry from time to time. (P.M.)

My mother was always competing with my family for attention. She simply refused to fit in. This made me angry. We all wanted her to be happy and to be part of the family. She just refused. (V.T).

I told her once, "You know you are very depressing to live with at times because you have no happiness. There's no joy. Think of the people who have no one. You live with us, your son and daughters come to visit all the time. Learn to appreciate what you have." She is very dependent. She won't make a decision. This is surprising to me. I always thought she was very strong and independent. She ran the house, took care of the home and all. She's not the person I remember. (S.L.)

When my father died, I felt little if any sadness. I remember him mainly as an emotionally abusive drunk. I assumed my mother would feel the same way. I thought, "At last she is free." When just the opposite happened and she seemed to fall apart, I became very angry at her. I remember thinking she just wanted to be a foolish martyr. She was not the person I made her out to be and I felt lost and betrayed. The feeling of betrayal turned into anger. The anger was directed at her. (K.V.)

If you begin to feel this kind of anger, it may be time to get to know your parents as the people they really are instead of the image you had of them.

Ask your parent about the years you were growing up. Find out what scared them then and how they dealt with their fears. Ask them why they never told you about their fears before. You will probably find out that they are afraid of the same types of things you are now afraid of for your family. Ask them about what they fear now and what you can do to help them with these fears.

There are many things, as fairly young, healthy adults, that we take for granted and don't even think about. Do you fear walking down stairs because you might fall, even in broad daylight? Probably not, but your parent may be unsure enough on his or her feet to have a real fear of falling. Do you fear falling asleep because you may not wake up? Again, probably not. This certainly was a fear of my mother's. As a result, she sometimes deprived herself of the sleep she needed. Do you fear the winter because "old cows and old people die in the winter?" Highly unlikely! However, this was a phrase my mother heard her old-country Irish mother use all the time. My mother, like her mother before her, became afraid and depressed in the winter. She lived for the first day of spring because she felt she would then have one more year to count on. These were things I hadn't really thought about until my mother started exhibiting all of these fears. Once I understood why she did and said some of the things she did, it was easier to help instead of just getting frustrated and angry.

Getting to know your parents as people as opposed to parents will help you overcome anger at the apparent weaknesses. You may also find out a lot about why you think and react as you do.

I finally just realized that she had emotional problems that had never been dealt with. She really couldn't control how she behaved. (V.T.)

I have always felt that emotional illness is no less real than physical illness. It just seems to carry a kind of stigma as if the person who was emotionally ill were bad. My mother was not a bad person. She was a sick person. (P.M).

It took a long time, but I finally came to realize that my father was my mother's reason for living. He gave her a focus. Her job was to take care of him because he was so needy. But she was just as needy as he was. She needed someone else to give her life meaning. She was co-dependent. This realization came as a real shock and threw my world into a tailspin. I had to ask myself if I was doing the same thing. Was I looking to other people to give my life meaning? Mom didn't seem to exist as a whole person after my father's death. Would the same thing happen to me? (K.V.)

Anger at Your Partner

You and your partner may find yourselves at odds quite a bit at first when a parent(s) moves in. Adjustment takes time. Your partner may resent some of the time and attention that your parents are now getting that previously was given to your family. As time passes, you will generally be able to reach happy mediums where time is concerned. Expect, however, to give up some free time to your parents' needs.

When new people are added to a family, whether it be a new baby or elderly parents, the family dynamics have to change. Nothing stays the same. Expect a certain amount of friction as each member of the family—old and new—learns to mesh his or her wants and needs with the newly formed group. Perhaps your children are used to you driving them wherever they want to go. They may have to learn to arrange rides for themselves from time to time or learn to use public transportation. If you and your spouse are in the habit of going out one night a week, your parents will have to learn to respect that or arrange to have their own company on the nights you want to go out. If your supper time and that of your parents varies widely, you may all have to compromise and find a midpoint that everyone can be happy with.

All of these types of changes and adjustments take time and patience to figure out. Remind everyone involved that the goal is to meet as many of everyone's needs and wants as possible and that cooperation is essential.

You may find your partner becoming very critical of your parents' need for attention. This is not necessarily out of jealousy. Any adult raised in a family system understands the influence that parents can exert over their children. If your parents appear to be reasserting that influence, your partner may have a very real cause for concern. It is very easy to fall back into the roles we played as we grew up. It is also very hard to tell your parents that they must stand in line for your time, just like everyone else in the family.

When my husband started showing anger at my parents' attitudes, he was reacting to concern for what he felt was unfair treatment of me. He resented anyone mistreating his wife, even her own parents. Since I had been raised by them, I was more used to how they reacted and behaved in different situations. I did not necessarily see their behavior as mistreatment. I might get angry at them, but I would also get angry with my husband because I didn't feel they had done anything terribly wrong. He and I were raised differently, with different expectations placed on us by our families. He was using his background to judge our circumstances. Of course, his was the only background he could use. I was using a different set of rules altogether. We did not see eye to eye on many situations that came up and frustration definitely started to build. A simple example of these types of frustrations was my mother's habit of waking me in the night. My husband felt that she was being selfish in doing this. When my husband was young, his mother had a tendency to believe that if she was up, everyone should be up. She would wake everyone when she got up because that was the way she was. My mother, on the other hand, always enjoyed sleeping late on her days off and would take naps, if possible, when we were younger. She hated it if someone woke her unnecessarily and never made us get up early on our days off if we didn't want to and there was no special reason to. When my mother lived with us, she did start waking me almost every night. Although I was not thrilled with this turn of events, I felt my mother wouldn't wake me unless she felt it was necessary. In most cases, there was, in fact, no emergency. She was lonely and afraid. Loneliness and fear can be very strong motivators. My husband was using his mother's past behavior to judge my mother's behavior. The situations were different and the people were different, but it is hard to separate our past experiences of our own families from those of our partners' families. As I got more tired, he got more angry. As my mother's health worsened, her ability to sleep through the night diminished even more. We finally solved the problem of interrupted sleep by hiring a nurse's aide to sit with my mother through the night. As long as someone was there, she was able to relax and sleep some. The whole situation, though, did cause friction between me and my husband until we found a solution—the nurse's aide—that satisfied all of our needs.

Dogs Get Mad, People Get Angry

As I mentioned before, I have a tendency to write lists and ask myself questions. I used the following questions to help in clarifying my thoughts and feelings:

1. What do you see as the problem? Answer in detail, point for point.

2. What do you think is causing the problem?

3. Why do you think the people involved are acting as they are?

4. List all (no matter how radical they may seem) possible solutions you see to the problem.

5. Reread your list from number 4. Cross out any solutions that cannot possibly be used.

6. Reread the remaining solutions. Rewrite the ones that seem most reasonable and workable.

7. Do you think that this problem can be avoided in the future? How?

8. Who needs to do the most changing in this situation?

9. If you are not the one who needs to make allowances, how can you help the person who does to make it as easy as possible?

10. If you are the one who needs to make changes, who can help you do this and how can they help?

Using the Questions

Numbers 4 and 5 from the above questions are very important. Anger often stems from frustration. It can be very frustrating to feel that everyone is pressing you to act in a certain way. Once you become overworked or overwrought, it is hard to keep a sense of perspective. By listing even the most outlandish solutions, you can start to get your sense of humor back and see the problem for what it is, a temporary irritation that probably does have a simple solution.

For example, let's say you have two school-aged children fairly involved in several activities; you or your spouse or both hold down full-time jobs; and you have your healthy but lonely mother with you. On any given day, your kids need to be taken to one or two sports activities, your spouse has had a rough day, you feel rushed, and mother is feeling neglected.

You rush in from work and start to collect the kids for their practices, making sure they have whatever equipment is needed. It does not matter what age they are, you still ask them if they have everything. If they don't you probably go into high gear to get the things they need and get them out the door. At this point, your spouse volunteers to take the kids or start dinner, whichever you prefer. You elect to take the kids. Your spouse heads for the kitchen.

Mom now enters and announces that she needs you to take her to an appointment which she did not tell you about previously. You ask why she didn't forewarn you, and she says it slipped her mind, but it is important and can't be cancelled. You cannot get your mother to her appointment and your kids to their practices and have everyone there on time. You go to the kitchen to ask your partner to take one or the other.

Dinner has been started. Your spouse reminds you that you chose to take the kids and is irritated that plans are being changed and everyone is getting upset about being late. Finally, your partner turns off the stove and takes the kids. You take your mother and end up waiting quite a while for her. When she is done, she is in a good mood and says she'll take you out to dinner since you missed, as did everyone else, dinner at home. You, however, are at this point ready to tear your hair out. You are tired and crabby. And when the kids come home from practice, they're going to be hungry and you'll feel obligated to get them dinner. You snap at your mother, she sulks, you all get home and sit around in a fairly black mood for the rest of the evening.

No one is happy. You feel that everyone expects too much of you. Your kids are irritated because they were late due to Grandma's last-minute demand. Your partner feels abused because he or she was trying to carry part of the load and still ended up in an argument. Your mother feels that you are being unfair to get mad at her since she has to make appointments in the evening because you work outside the home during the day.

Some Answers for the Above

If this type of scenario goes on with any amount of regularity, and it does in many homes, you can use the questions to help find a solution. Questions 4 and 5 can help by being a pressure valve and letting you blow off some steam. A possible list of solutions for question 4 may be:

1. Run away.

2. Sell the kids.

3. Insist that all activities or appointments be announced at least 48 hours in advance.

4. Find a new husband for Mom.

5. Hire a cook.

6. Hire a hit man.

7. Buy a large write-on calendar and put it in a central place. Have everyone write his or her week's activities on the calendar no later than Sunday night of each week.

8. Slow down.

9. Ask the kids for suggestions.

10. Ask Mom for suggestions.

11. Prearrange the cook and cleanup crew for each meal.

Now that you have listed possible solutions, right down to selling the kids and matchmaking for your mother, go back and cross out the ones that really can't be used or are beyond your power to accomplish. When you finish, your list may look like this:

1. Run away.

2. Sell the kids.

3. Insist that all activities or appointments be announced at least 48 hours in advance.

4. Find a new husband for Mom.

5. Hire a cook.

6. Hire a hit man.

7. Buy a large write-on calendar and put it in a central place. Have everyone write his or her week's activities on the calendar no later than Sunday night of each week.

8. Slow down.

9. Ask the kids for suggestions.

10. Ask Mom for suggestions.

11. Prearrange the cook and cleanup crew for each meal.

The possible solutions left on the list can be accomplished and will probably solve the problem. By writing numbers 1, 2, 4, and 6, however, you have acknowledged your extreme frustration and given vent to your feelings. By writing them down, you can see that the problem really isn't that drastic and can be solved. By crossing them out, you are giving yourself the option of physically rejecting the idea that the problem is insurmountable.

Anger at Yourself
Yes, you do not escape being the victim of your own anger. One of the most common causes of anger is frustration. On any given day, with or without aging parents, we can become frustrated because we feel inadequate to the task at hand. We may wonder why we are always rushed, or why we can't be more organized, or why we can't find time to do the things we enjoy, or even why we can't seem to remember to empty the litter box.

You and I live in a very busy world. We are surrounded by distractions and upsets. We can make schedules until they come out our ears and still find that we were pushed off course by an unexpected event or emergency. These everyday disruptions can cause us to feel frustrated and angry at our inability to keep to a schedule or to accomplish as much as we wanted. When we add the responsibility of caring for aged or sickly parents to our list of things to do, we may find the frustration mounting faster than we can cope with it. These frustrations can then be turned into anger at ourselves.

In my case, this happened very early on. I worked full-time at this point as a free-lance writer, and had always worked throughout my married life. Although I keep a clean house, I am not a fanatic about it. Schedules were, to say the very least, loose. About this I had made peace in my own mind. But when my parents moved in, I felt the need to keep the house spotless at all times. Company would drop in unexpectedly to visit my parents. I was not used to this. No one, neither my parents, my family, nor the company that dropped in, ever suggested that the house wasn't clean. This was in my mind only. It became an obsession. My house wasn't clean enough.

This does not mean that I then spent every waking moment cleaning. What it did mean is that I began to spend an inordinate amount of time fretting about it. It began to interfere with my work. I became angry with myself because I wasn't doing my work as smoothly as I was used to, and the house was actually messier than before I started worrying about it. I became more angry with myself. This anger started to spread to other members of the family. At this point, I no longer felt that I could write very well, I was a lousy housekeeper, and a rag to boot. This is not the description of a nice person. So, I was no longer a nice person.

This frustration and anger was not really something that my family could help me with. They didn't see anything wrong with the house. They didn't see me as an incompetent writer. My husband did, in fact, think of me as a nice person. Strange, perhaps, but nice.

The problem, of course, was that I was feeling overwhelmed and frightened that I couldn't live up to the responsibilities I felt were mine. My first mistake was assuming that the responsibility for everything was mine. In order to snap myself out of this destructive anger/frustration cycle, I questioned each of the problem areas and how I was feeling about them.

Q. What is the worst possible thing that can happen if the house is dirty?

A. We could get bugs. It could stink. The health department could come and they'll show us on the nightly news while the health-department workers shovel out the scum. Everyone would know that my house is a mess.

Q. How long would it take us to get to health-department stage?

A. About five years.

Q. What is the worst possible thing that could happen if I became totally dysfunctional and couldn't write another word?

A. We could go broke and end up in the poorhouse.

Q. Would this happen before health-department stage?

A. Yes!

Q. Which is more important?

A. Staying out of the poorhouse.

Solution: Forget the house and get back to work. You have five years before you'll end up on the nightly news. Anyway maybe you could write a story about it.

The irrational bent to the questions and answers helped to snap me out of the corner my frustration and anger had put me in. It made me realize that I was letting my imagination get totally out of hand. My family has always helped with the house. It was my notion that it wasn't clean enough. Giving in to the thought that everything was my responsibility effectively froze me in my tracks. However, no one but myself thought that everything was my responsibility. My frustration and anger led to my feeling sorry for myself. Martyrs have no fun. Martyrs do not allow anyone else to have fun. Misery does indeed love company.

Sources of Help

I learned one invaluable lesson from this very unexpected crash into the world of frustration, anger, and self-pity. That is: People want to help. If you are feeling overwhelmed, ask for help. Don't sit back and expect the people around you to know what you need or want. They are not mind readers. Ask and you probably will receive.

At the time that this was going on with me, there certainly was more work in the house. I did feel guilty about the extra burdens placed on my family. There were more people going in and out of the house. I was having trouble building a new work schedule around the added work. All of this was true. The part that wasn't true at all was that I had to handle everything myself.

One of the most psychologically refreshing things I did for myself at this time was to tell my brother and sister how I felt and suggest that they supply a cleaning service to help me keep the house up. They not only agreed, they thought it was a wonderful idea. They were feeling a bit guilty themselves for not being able to be of more help. By paying for the cleaning service, they knew they were giving me something I really needed for myself. We all came out of it better off and closer as a family.

Using Anger Constructively

The anger that can appear directed at the situation and all the players involved can help you get a better feeling for who you are, who your parents are, and how you function as a family. Anger is a sign that something is wrong. It's like pain or a fever is to your body: a sign. If it lasts just a short time and then disappears, it was probably just a minor problem that didn't need a lot of solving, like a head cold that runs its course and leaves. But if you cannot shake the anger, if it keeps coming back to the point that you start taking it out on the people around you, it is serious and must be dealt with.

Don't suppress it by trying to ignore it. Find out what is causing it. Talk to the people around you. Find out if they are feeling the same way or if you're the only one who seems to be having a problem. Work out a set of questions or guidelines to help you walk through the anger to its source. Ask for help.

Finally, do not be afraid to go outside your home for help. Many times when people are all tied up in the same problem, they cannot help each other or themselves. The problem is too close and affects everyone. Many hospitals now have home health-care departments. These departments usually include support groups for caregivers. Join one of these groups. Talk to other people who are in the same position. You will find out that your problems and their problems sound quite alike. They will understand your frustrations and anger and help you to work on them. Do not feel that you're a failure because you can't handle the emotional or physical stress of taking care of your aging parents by yourself. No one can. Get all the help you can. As Karen did:

> I thought I could make my mother happy. All I really accomplished on my own was to make myself feel incompetent and angry. I called the Social Services Department at Mother's hospital looking for help in solving her problems. They did make many helpful suggestions, but to my astonishment, they suggested more things for me than for her. One of their suggestions was that I join Adult Children of Alcoholics (ACOA). I did and I couldn't believe how much it helped. The other people at the meetings sounded as if they were raised in my home with me. They understood. It was also suggested that my mother join Al-Anon to help her understand her life with an alcoholic. She refused. The minute my father died, he became a saint. She was in total denial about him and about her life. (K.V.)

Regardless of whether Karen's mother got help or not, the most important thing for Karen was that she got help. She learned, as I did, that we are not alone unless we choose to be.

Review

Learn to look at anger realistically and find its cause.

Understand that you may become angry at the entire situation, but that this anger usually passes on its own. It may not, however. If it doesn't you will need to get help.

Anger at your parents may be caused by their inability to live up to your ideas of what they should be or do. Look at them as people as well as parents.

Remember that your partner is probably more interested in your welfare than that of your parents. He or she may become angry at the situation or at your parents. Try to see the situation through your partner's eyes.

Look squarely at problems that make you angry. Write down the problem(s) and all possible solutions. Writing things down helps to defuse them.

Try not to be too hard on yourself. If you become angry at yourself, remember you are just one human being. You are not expected to do everything by yourself.

Get all the help you can. Talk to people. Ask your siblings for support even if that support takes the shape of something nice for you rather than something for your parents.

Find a caregiver support group and join it.

5

KNOWING YOUR EXPECTATIONS

My father called home from work on one of my birthdays, maybe the seventh or eighth, I'm not sure any more and asked my mom if she thought I would like new pj's for my birthday. She asked me. I promptly said yes and went into a frenzy of expectation for the rest of the day. I had no idea what pj's were, but I was sure they must be something strange, wonderful, and mysterious if I didn't know what they were.

It never occurred to me to ask someone what pj's were or even to wonder what kinds of things my dad would consider appropriate for a young girl's birthday. I was just sure it would be something wonderful. It might even be a type of pony I had never heard of. When, in fact, pj's turned out to be pajamas, I was crushed. I had expected something wonderful! What I got was a very nice pair of cotton pajamas. There was nothing wrong with the pajamas. What was wrong were my expectations. I ruined the gift of the pajamas by spending too much time building up my expectations. Instead of being happy with what I did get, I was unhappy because of what I didn't get.

I have done this to myself thousands of times over the years—ruined the reality by having unrealistic expectations. The building of expectations may be exciting, but the crash that occurs when reality refuses to match expectations can be devastating.

What do you expect to happen when your parents move in? This is a vital question to ask yourself. False expectations can ruin you and your relationship with your parents. Having false expectations of future behavior is one way of depriving a person of the right to be himself or herself.

There are usually a lot of expectations connected with the situation of moving a parent into your home. You may expect your parents to be as they were when you were young. They probably won't be. You may expect your parents to be grateful for your kindness and understanding in moving them in. I have heard many stories of people being crushed because they can't seem to do enough for their parent; the more they do, the more the parent demands.

If your parent is ill, you may expect him or her to rally now that they are under your care. This may or may not happen. Be prepared for the opposite to happen. The process of moving out of their own home and into your home may signal the beginning of the end for them. They may become despondent and much worse physically and emotionally. It is a blow for any adult to have to admit that he or she can no longer cope with daily living without help.

You may expect your parents to be overjoyed to be with their grandchildren on a daily basis. This also may not happen. The strain of having small children or even teenagers around again may be too much for them to cope with. You may also find that they do not agree with your methods of child-rearing.

Beware of expectations. They can be killers. Use the sets of questions that follow to get an idea of what your expectations are and what your parents' expectations are.

What Can I Expect?

What kinds of activities do you expect your parents to do around your house?

Do they know that you are expecting this of them?

What kinds of activities do your parents expect to do around your house?

Which of their needs do you expect them to care for themselves?

Which of their needs do you expect to take care of?

How do you expect your parents to act toward your children? Your partner?

What evidence do you have for their expected behavior toward your children and partner?

What will you do if they cannot or will not live up to your expectations as far as activities are concerned?

What will you do if they cannot or will not behave toward your family as you expect them to?

How long do you expect your parents to live?

How long do you expect them to be able to function with little or no help?

What will you do if they fall far short of the time you expected them to function with little or no help?

Under what circumstances will you consider a nursing home?

What Is Your Attitude?

How do you expect your parents to react to moving into your home?

Do you expect their attitude toward you and your family to stay the same, or to change once they have moved in?

What do you expect your brothers' and sisters' attitudes to be about your parents moving in?

What do you expect your partner's attitude to be?

What are you prepared to do if your partner's attitude toward your parents isn't all you would like it to be?

Expectations and the Sick Parent

If your parents were healthy in their youth and middle age, and you remember them as vital, in fairly good humor, and fairly easy to deal with, you may be in for a big shock if they become seriously ill. Most of us have been raised in a kind of Walt Disney world where wild animals are cute and tame, and sick people are long-suffering and gentle. Neither of the above is necessarily true. Wild animals will attack if they feel threatened. Some sick people are neither long-suffering nor gentle. Sick people sometimes seem to attack those around them. There are many reasons for this. A lot of them have to do with expectations.

They Never Expected to Get Sick

The first reason for the fact that sick people are sometimes less than pleasant to deal with is that they are probably shocked and angry at the fact that they actually got sick in the first place. A vigorous 50-year-old cannot picture himself or herself as a frail 80-year-old. Sickness, especially debilitating sickness, takes people by surprise. They become understandably frightened and angry at their circumstances.

Anger looks for an outlet. The person closest to the sick person often becomes that outlet. If you take over the care of a sick parent, you may find yourself confused and become angry that you are being attacked even as you try your best to be helpful. Keep reminding yourself that the sick parent is probably attacking the circumstances and not you. On your good days this will help, on bad days it might just get you through the day.

> My mother-in-law found fault with everything we did or didn't do. We stayed up too late. We went to bed too early. We bothered her when she was trying to sleep. We didn't spend enough time with her. We never went out and enjoyed ourselves. We left her alone too much. She said there was an underlying tension in the house that made her uncomfortable; she assumed my wife and I weren't getting along. Actually it was her. We didn't know what to do since nothing we did seemed right to her. She was angry at everything and everyone. She was angry at the world. (P.M.)

If you find yourself in this situation, the first thing you might want to do is ask your sick parent why he or she is attacking. You may be surprised by the answers you get. If you expected your parent to get better under your care, it is a distinct possibility that he or she was expecting the same thing. Your parent may have come into your home expecting to get better. If, in fact, he or she gets no better or actually gets worse, the disappointment he or she feels could easily turn into anger. If you were doing all that could be done, then surely, your parent might feel he or she would be getting better.

Consciously, this line of thought does not seem rational. It is not, however, rational thought you will be dealing with. Major changes in life-style can and often do evoke emotional storms that take everyone by surprise. Sometimes just talking about what is going on and how you both feel about it can ease the tension and help both you and your parent take a more realistic view of what to expect.

They Don't Feel Well

Another important reason that sick people are sometimes hard to deal with is that they just don't feel well. They may be in severe pain at the worst, or severe discomfort at the least. In any case, they don't feel as they think they should. It is very hard to be in a good mood when you are in pain and discomfort. They know what hurts and may expect other people to be constantly aware of their problems.

For example, my mother had a tendency to get short of breath if she turned to the left. At times, I would forget this and place things on her left. She would get angry at me for what she saw as my inconsideration. Depending on the day and my mood—even people who are trying to take care of others are human and do have an occasional mood—I would either just ignore her anger and move whatever I had put down, or I would silently fume because she didn't seem to be aware of all the things I had done properly.

You may also be faced with fury if you try to empathize and tell your parent that you know how he or she feels. You may be trying to be nice and understanding, but your parent may just blow up in your face and tell you that you have no idea how it feels. The retort will probably be right. It is extremely hard, if not impossible, for a healthy person to imagine being in constant pain or discomfort. I cannot for a second imagine not being able to breathe and the terror that must bring. I tried. I tried very hard. I even held my breath for as long as I could. That didn't work. I ran as fast as I could for as long as I could until I was gasping for breath. That helped, but all along I knew that I would in fact be able to get my breath. My mother never knew if she would be able to regain her breath. Sometimes she could and sometimes she couldn't. There is a huge difference there.

Ask your parent to describe how he or she is feeling. Even if your parent has a chronic illness, he or she will probably have good days and bad days. Remind your parents that you are not always able to tell if they are feeling badly on any given day and that you need his or her help in knowing what to do to help.

Make it clear, though, that you will take their word for how they are feeling. It is not unusual for an elderly person to say he or she feels fine when, in fact, they don't. This is sometimes due to an effort on the sick parent's part not to be a burden. Sometimes, though, it is because the parent feels you should know how he or she feels without being told. This is a situation that should be avoided. Remind your parents that you are busy and you are not a mind reader. You need to be told if they need something done for them.

They May Know They Are Dying

This is a very important thing to keep in mind. You as your parent's child probably will hold out hope for recovery until the very end. Your severely ill parent will probably shift between hoping for recovery and wishing it were over. If your parent is frail and in ill health, he or she is probably painfully aware that things just aren't ever going to get better, only worse, and they are probably terrified at the idea of it getting worse. This does not tend to put a person in a good mood. It is hard to ignore for any length of time. For my mother, getting worse meant more and longer bouts with her inability to breath. She spent more and more time in the hospital on ventilators. The doctors held out no hope for improvement. Each episode on a ventilator got longer and it became harder and harder for her to get off once she was on one. Sara's (S.L.) mother is experiencing increasing difficulty in walking and has more frequent bouts of angina. She, too, is becoming more and more worried about what will happen if her health deteriorates further. Will she be able to walk at all? Will the angina pain come more frequently and last longer? Jane's mother, on the other hand, grew less and less aware of her worsening condition as time went by and did not seem bothered by what was happening to her. Kathy's father is quite well so he spends little time fretting about his future health.

If your parents are frail or sickly, they will probably fight further debility with every ounce of strength they have. This leaves them little physical or emotional strength left for the niceties of life. Bear with them. Try to put yourself in their place. It isn't easy, but it will help you bear up under bad moods or the feeling that they do not appreciate anything you do for them. They are engaged in a life and death battle and they know it.

Expect Everything to Work Out for the Best

The one expectation that we can have when bringing our parents into our homes is to expect everything to work out for the best in the long run. Whether our parents are basically healthy or are in increasingly failing health, we can assume that everyone will be doing whatever they can to make the best of the situation. We can't expect everyone to be happy all of the time. We can't expect everyone to be grateful all of the time. We can't even expect everyone to be cordial all of the time. We can expect, though, that if we are all working together in a spirit of love we will make it through and be better for the experience. We can expect to feel good about ourselves and about our family. We can expect our love and devotion to our parents to carry them and us through if times get rough. We can expect to be a better family for having tried to help those we love.

Review

Take time to think about your expectations about your parents. How do you expect your parents to feel and behave? How do you expect your family to feel and behave?

Ask your parents what they expect to be responsible for in your home.

Ask your parents what aspects of their care they expect you to be responsible for.

Don't expect a sick parent to get well just because they move in with you.

Don't expect your parents to be overjoyed because they move in.

Don't expect your love to overcome your parents' fears and pain, if they are sick.

Don't expect a sick person to be in a good mood.

Do expect to work everything out in the long run.

Do expect to be able to handle whatever situations occur.

Do expect your family to be better and stronger for having worked together to help a loved one.

6
FEAR

No one wants to deal with fear. In my interviews, the subject came up again and again. What is there to fear about your parents moving into your home? Many things. Some are well-founded fears, others aren't.

Your fears will probably have a lot to do with the state of your parents' health and the state of your relationship with them. If you and your parent(s) get along well, and that parent is in relatively good health, you will probably only experience minor fears about how everyone will get along and if both your family and your parent(s) will be happy with the new living arrangements.

If, on the other hand, your parent(s) is in failing health, you may be faced with a whole different set of fears:

I'm afraid of everything. I'm a chicken. I get real panicked when she has these attacks. I don't know what to do. (S.L.)

The only time I would experience fear was when I was taking her to the hospital because I never knew how sick she really was. (V.T.)

Up to the time when I placed my mother in a nursing home, I was somewhat fearful for her future. I was afraid she would never be happy. When my mother continued her program of starvation and dehydration in the nursing home, I think the fear was replaced by the certainty that she would eventually go too far and not be able to recover. At this point, I think I began to mourn her coming death. (P.M.)

I fear my father's passing. I love him. I depend a great deal on him. I guess that's my biggest fear. I don't know what I'd do without him. I also worry about him becoming ill. My father is a caretaker. I would miss him terribly if he were gone. (K.H.)

The following list summarizes the things people seemed most afraid of:

Fear for the parent's health

Fear that a nursing home will become necessary

Fear of the parent's death

Fear of finding the parent dead

Fear of personality problems that might arise

Fear that the parents won't like their new home

Fear that the arrangement will put too much physical and emotional strain on the family

Fear that the arrangement will put too much of a monetary strain on the family

Fear that siblings will not take any responsibility

Fear for the parent's future should something happen to you

What Do I Do about My Fears?

One of the most effective ways to deal with fear is to talk it out. This usually works as long as you know what it is you fear. Different people fear different things. You will probably not find yourself afraid of all of the situations listed. There may be things that you fear that don't appear on the list. Some things that you don't fear today, given your circumstances and that of your parents, may become a fear in the future if your circumstances or that of your parents changes. Certainly, if your parent(s) is fairly healthy and well adjusted, you probably won't have the same types of fears as someone whose parent(s) is frail or suffering a serious illness. The first thing you need to do in either case, though, to start combating your fears is to find out what they are.

Am I afraid of sickness?

If I am, what possible reasons might I have for this fear?

Am I afraid of death?

What about death frightens me—the fear of the unknown, the finality of it, or the actual physical occurrence?

What do I expect to find should my parent die in his or her sleep?

Who can I talk to in order to find out what to expect to see should my parent die in my home?

Are we financially secure or insecure?

Are we able to pick up some of the medical bills if my parents cannot?

What chores would I be hesitant to do for my parent's upkeep should he or she become seriously ill?

How do I feel about incontinent adults?

What would happen to my parent should something happen to me?

I always considered myself a risk-taker. Maybe the word "brave" didn't actually enter into my idea of myself, but I guess that's how I felt about myself. I had been courageous enough to fight alcoholism and go on to be a productive human being. My husband and I had had some serious emotional and financial problems over the years, but we faced them head-on and did what needed to be done. I don't remember as an adult ever feeling very afraid or insecure. That all changed, though, after my mother moved in with us. It seemed that overnight I became afraid of everything. I was afraid of the future—both Mother's and mine. I was afraid I wouldn't be able to cope with her. I was afraid she would sicken and die like my father. On the other hand, I was terrified that I'd wake up one morning and find her dead. At times, the fear was almost alive. It was overwhelming. I couldn't handle it alone. (K.V.)

Common Fears
Sickness.

Most healthy people who are not involved in the practice of medicine are at least mildly afraid of sick people. You probably learned to deal with this fear where your kids were concerned. You dealt with injuries and illness when they happened and didn't spend an inordinate amount of time in between worrying about what your reaction would be the next time. Many mothers and fathers, for example, gagged over their first few diapers or retched along with a vomiting child. You get over this, though; diapers become another part of the day, and you learn to help a vomiting child without retching. Even if you never learn to control the impulse to retch while helping a person who is vomiting, you at least learn to go right on helping while you retch. The first time your child falls and really cuts himself or herself, you may have felt panic, but you controlled it and did what needed to be done. You probably did not stay up nights, however, worrying about the next time your child might fall.

If you have more than one child, or even one child who is physically very active, you've probably learned to take injuries in stride. You empathize with the child, you do what needs to be done, and you get on with it. Panic is then reserved for major emergencies. Luckily those are usually very few.

You may, indeed, find yourself worrying more if you are dealing with a chronic problem rather than a random accident or illness. If your child or partner has asthma or diabetes, for example, you may find yourself fretting more and consciously monitoring their activities in order to avoid emergency situations. Long before my parents moved into our home, my husband developed a severe allergy to a type of stinging insect called a Yellow Jacket. They look like bees but they are really a type of hornet. He was stung three times in our backyard and twice at work. Each time he was stung, the reaction got worse. The last time, he almost died. I found myself watching him whenever he went into the backyard. My anxiety level increased drastically in the summer. When this problem first surfaced, I would get panicky if he went into the yard because I didn't know if I would be able to get to him in time if he was stung. I did get over this fear to a point after talking to the doctors and learning how to administer the injections he kept in the house in case of emergency. However, it is a real problem that can't be ignored entirely, and still causes anxiety to this day if there are Yellow Jackets around. We did, however, learn to live with it and refused to let it control our actions.

This is the key to dealing with fears about sick parents. Assume that you will learn to deal with them just as you learned to deal with other members of your family. Sickness does happen. You may find yourself in a position that requires you to place and remove the equivalent of adult diapers on your parents. You grow as used to this as you did with your children's. When serious emergencies arise, and they might, you will probably deal with them in the same way you have taught yourself to deal with your children's.

You quickly size up the situation, determine whether it is something you can handle or not, and if not, call for someone who can handle it. Remember, most, if not all, communities provide emergency ambulance service.

Taking specific action can also allay some of your fears. Call your local Red Cross chapter and find out when they offer emergency training. Learn how to do CPR. You will probably never have to use these skills, but you will feel more confident knowing them.

If your parent has a specific medical problem, learn all you can about the condition and how to deal with emergencies related to this condition. In my husband's case, I learned how to administer the injection he would need immediately if he were stung. My father has diabetes. He deals with this himself. He gives himself insulin shots. I am not required to do that. I know how to, though, just in case an emergency arises. We took the time to read about diabetes and the signs to look for if something seems to be wrong.

Talk to your parents' doctors. If your parents object, be firm. Remind them that you are the one who will be expected to handle emergencies and that you need to know exactly what you may be dealing with. Make it clear to the doctors that you need to know everything there is to know about your parents' health. If the doctors object, be firm. You are the one who is going to have to talk to them in an emergency, so it is essential that you be comfortable with relaying symptoms and conditions.

Some doctors want only to deal with the patient. They understandably want their elderly patients to stay alert and in charge of their own health-care programs for as long as they can. Sometimes, though, this becomes unreasonable. There should be no surprises. Insist that all possible health-care problems are made known to you and, if possible, any home emergency methods you can take.

I started telling the doctor her [mother's] symptoms and mentioned that I gave her a squirt of medicine from her atomizer. He pounced on that. I shouldn't be doing that.

She should do it for herself. I reminded him that I had already told him that her arms were numb and she couldn't handle it. So he said that if she couldn't squirt it herself, she should have pills instead. I was sick and tired of fighting. I told him that was fine. Prescribe the pills but don't cancel the atomizer. Someone from my family is always with her and the atomizer works faster. I didn't bother to tell him that if she couldn't lift her arms to use the atomizer, she certainly wouldn't be able to get the top off the bottle of medicine. I'm sick of fighting with him. He wants her to do it for herself. She won't. He just refuses to acknowledge that, so I get caught in the middle. (S.L.)

In the course of talking to people with sickly parents, this problem seemed to arise again and again—an apparent lack of understanding or an unwillingness on the part of the doctor to take all of the parent's health conditions into account and to deal with family members. In my mother's case, one of the doctors seemed to have no patience or understanding when he dealt with her. He talked to her as if he was talking to a twenty-year-old with a passing illness. This wasn't the case. It sometimes took me days to calm her down after she saw him. We changed doctors and I went to heroic lengths to make sure she wasn't taken to the hospital he practiced from if there was an emergency. You may need to do the same thing. If your parent is of advanced age and in ill health, try to find a doctor who specializes in geriatric medicine and is fully aware of all that that entails. Ask questions. Don't be put off by a brusque attitude. If the doctor persists in ignoring your questions and concerns or those of your parent, find a different doctor. You have your parent's best interest in mind, the doctor should also have your parent's best interest in mind. This means that the doctor should welcome both you and your parent as part of your parent's health-care team.

The Future.

Fear of the future was mentioned by many people. Those who had healthy parents feared future illness. Those who had sick parents feared the worsening of health. Some feared the possibility of needing a nursing home. One, who had no brothers or sisters, feared for her father's future should something happen to her.

> I'm an only child. I fear for my father's future should something happen to me. He has three sisters and a brother. I think that they are good people and would do what they could, but they are no longer young either. I don't think he would stay here if something happened to me. I don't think he would feel comfortable doing that. But that, too, worries me because I think he would miss the children terribly and I don't know who would take care of him if he became ill. (K.H.)

Although there is little that can actually be done about the future, acknowledging your fears and looking at them realistically can help. Think back over your own life and the things you feared the most in the past. You will probably find that the things that you most feared—the future disasters that you fretted and worried about—never came to pass.

> My biggest fear with my mother-in-law was that her condition would continue to get worse and my wife would refuse to put her in a nursing home. She was already bedridden and needed a tremendous amount of care. My wife kept thinking that she would get better. I didn't. I was beginning to think that she was enjoying all the attention she was getting and had decided to just let people take care of her. I couldn't see any kind of normal life for our future. I was feeling very trapped by the whole situation. I needn't have looked so far in the future. She passed away long before I expected her to. (P.M.)

How many times did you worry and fret about something that you thought was going to happen, only to have a completely different problem arise that you didn't even consider a possibility? This type of thing happens all the time in people's lives. We worry, we plan, we fret, we lose sleep, and then the catastrophe we were sure was about to hit never happens. You then find yourself thinking, "Whatever did I let myself get all wound up for?" Then, of course, the next possible catastrophe rears its head and we start the process all over again, usually with the same results.

This also applies to your worry for your parents. Most of the things you worry about the most just won't happen. Don't bother to worry about them. On the other hand, sometimes concentrating on possible plans of action for future emergencies can help diminish fears. If you're busy with logical problem solving, you generally don't have the time for undue worry.

Look at Some Nursing Homes

Consider the idea that your parent may some day need a nursing home for his or her own good. Spend some time checking out the nursing homes in your area. Ask the hospital at which your parent's doctor practices to recommend two or three nursing homes to you so you can visit them. Visit the nursing homes. Ask questions about health care, food, activities, and anything else that may be on your mind. Ask for a tour of the facilities.

> My mother needed constant care because of the Alzheimer's disease. I was able to keep her home, but it was getting harder and harder. When she started having small strokes and then heart problems, it became more and more obvious that I would not be able to give her the level of care she needed. During one hospitalization, my sisters and I agreed that it was time to look for a nursing home. We found several and asked many questions. None of us had really ever thought a nursing home would be necessary, and we had no idea what to expect. Although by this

time my mother had no idea where she was or who we were, we found it hard to think of her any place but in her own home. As it turned out, she passed away in the hospital and never did go to a nursing home. (J.M.)

Ask About Possible Future Health Problems

If your parent, like mine, has a progressive degenerative disease, ask his or her doctor what to expect and how debilitated the average person with this disease becomes. If your parent does have a chronic condition, chances are he or she is seeing a specialist who concentrates on that condition. That specialist should be able to give a fairly detailed description of what to expect under normal circumstances.

Talk with your parent about his or her expectations for the future. You may find that your parent has already thought about it and has a mental cut-off point at which he or she will ask to go to a nursing home. Generally your parents have a better idea of what they want and what they expect to have happen than you think. I was sure that my mother would never, ever consider going into a nursing home. I was wrong. While we waited for the ambulance the last time she went to the hospital, she told me she wanted me to find a nursing home for her. She was becoming more and more uncomfortable in my home because I couldn't give her the care she really needed. She wanted to be somewhere where there were people up and alert all night in case of emergency. She also was getting very concerned with my health. She felt her health problems were putting too much pressure on me. This all came as a complete shock to me. I didn't think she had ever considered the possibility of a nursing home and had been very hesitant to bring the subject up myself. Apparently she had been thinking about it for some time. I just never asked her how she felt on the subject. Don't think for your parents. Unless your parent's mental faculties are clearly diminished, they have the right to make their own life decisions. One of our jobs is to give them as many options as possible. Not to decide for them.

We live in an age in which medical technology can do wonders. People regularly recover from illnesses that a few short years ago would have most certainly been fatal. On the other hand, this same technology has also created problems never before thought of.

It is imperative that your parents decide before they become too ill to make their wishes known, just how much and what type of care they really want. This can be taken care of through the use of a living will. A living will is simply a document in which a person's preference for extended care is stated clearly for the benefit of the family and the medical authorities. A living will only comes into use if the person himself or herself is no longer able to communicate this information.

If a living will is in place before one of your parents becomes incapable of making his or her wishes known, the burden of decision is taken off the shoulders of an already grieving family.

My mother did not have a living will. She was, however, very clear about what she wanted each time she went to the hospital. Each time, until the last time, she said she wanted the respirator if she went into a respiratory crisis. She felt these crises were temporary and that the respirator was just an aid to get her through the crisis. The doctors in one of the hospitals she went to did not agree. They viewed the respirator as an heroic measure and didn't want to use it. I felt this was my mother's decision to make, and as long as she wanted to fight, she had the right.

The last time she went to the hospital, she specifically told the doctor that should she go into respiratory crisis, she didn't want the respirator. She was tired of fighting. She knew what she was doing. She had the right to make her own decisions.

Discuss the possibility of the use of a living will with your parents. Most people really don't want to be kept alive with machinery. The hospitals, however, are bound to do what they can to prolong life. If they have no instructions from the patient, they will proceed with whatever hospital policy dictates.

Ask your doctor or lawyer about living wills and how to go about using them. They can spare both you and your parents extra emotional crisis should emergencies strike.

Talk to the People Around You

People from very small families do have a real problem in the area of back-up in times of emergency. If, like Kathy (K.H.), you have no brothers or sisters who can step in if something happens to you, discuss the problem with your parent and with your partner. Do not think for other people. I am almost always wrong when I start assuming what other people will think or say. You may find that your partner has no intention of turning your parent out should something happen to you. You may also find that your parent would still be very comfortable living with your partner if something happened to you. Don't assume. Ask them what they think and how they feel about this situation. Also keep firmly in mind that unless you know you have a fatal illness, you will almost certainly outlive your parents.

What If?

Most of all, remember that fear cannot stay in the same room with a brave person. Don't fear the unknown. Yesterday was unknown the day before yesterday, but you got through it all right. In taking care of your parents, you are exhibiting the finest quality of the human being—the desire to help others. Fear cannot stand up before this kind of love and dedication.

Face each new situation on a daily basis, and tomorrow will take care of itself. You can "what if" yourself into an asylum, but it doesn't have to happen. If you looked at the worst possible happenstance it would have to be "what if the world ended tomorrow?" Well, what if? Then you'd have nothing to worry about. So every morning when you wake up, look outside and say, "Whew, it didn't end last night, so I guess I'd better get on with today."

Finally, on the subject of fear, I would like to borrow from the many self-help programs based on the Twelve Steps of Alcoholics Anonymous. There is no problem too big to handle one day at a time. Take care of today and tomorrow will take care of itself.

Death

Although death is probably one of everyone's biggest fears, while talking to people about taking care of their elderly parents, I found that their fears about death were very similar to my own. As reasonable adults, we understand the inevitability of death. Everyone dies. Death is natural. Most of the people I talked to really weren't that afraid that their parent(s) would die someday. They knew that they would. Many, in fact, had already lost one parent. Their worst fears, and mine, revolved around where and how they would die rather than if they would die.

> I'm not looking forward to it but I don't think I'm afraid of her dying. The thing that worries me the most is her dying at home. What would I do with the kids? I don't think I would want them to have to deal with it. At the hospital there are always people around. (S.L.)

Death at Home

This was probably the most pronounced fear about death expressed in the interviews and it was my worst fear. In today's society, most people have not been faced with the problem of a loved one dying at home. Terribly sick people go to the hospital to be cared for. Generally they die in the hospital. Of course, there are exceptions to this. People have sudden heart attacks, or sometimes the elderly do die in their sleep. Most people today, however, sicken, go to a hospital, and die there.

81

People fear the possibility of finding a loved one dead. It is a real fear that must be faced and dealt with. In our case, I was lucky. My husband, being a police officer in a large city, had dealt with death on many occasions. For many years he was a wagon man. It is the wagon or squadrol that is called to remove the bodies of those who die in their homes. He had seen death in the home many times and it did not scare him. Even when my parents were living in their own home, there were occasions when my mother was in the hospital and my father didn't answer the phone that my husband, rather than me, went to check on him. The reason? I was afraid I would find him dead. After all, he was in his eighties and was diabetic. Each time my mother entered the hospital, before they moved in with us, I would ask him to come and stay with us. He always refused. He felt I was treating him like a baby. However, on more than one occasion, the change in schedule and life-style brought on by my mother's absence caused him to forget his insulin. More than once we got to him just in time to avert real trouble.

After my parents moved in, I became very used to their sleeping habits and counted on them to start moving around and making noise at the same time every morning. If they, for one reason or another, slept later than usual, I would find myself making noise in the kitchen hoping to wake them, I admit, I'm a coward. I just didn't want to be the one to open the door and find them dead. It never happened. It probably won't happen to you either. If your parent has a chronic illness, he or she is probably very aware of exactly how they feel at any given moment. They often know when something is going wrong, and they probably don't want to hang around the house waiting for a disaster any more than you do.

The last time my mother went to the hospital, she seemed in fairly good shape. She wasn't. She knew her body was working up to an acute attack and she asked to be taken to the hospital before it hit. She knew she would feel safer in the hospital than at home if an attack was coming on. Your

82

parents may very well react in the same way. No one wants amateurs dealing with their lives in an emergency if they can get to the professionals they have come to count on. They will probably let you know immediately if they think something is going wrong with them.

She certainly doesn't wait around. At the first indication that anything is wrong, she yells for me. She has an intercom like the ones you put in a baby's room. I can always hear her. She calls me the second she thinks something is wrong. (S.L.)

If, however, your worst fears do come true and your parent dies at home, stay calm. Remind yourself that there is absolutely nothing you can do to help them now. Call your local emergency number. The members of your police and fire departments are trained to deal with this type of emergency. They know what needs to be done and will take over the minute they get to you. If it bothers you to go into the room, don't do it. It isn't necessary. It is not showing disloyalty or lack of love to simply leave the room, close the door, and wait for the people who know how to handle the situation. If you are alone in the house, don't be brave. Call a friend or neighbor to come and sit with you until your family can get there. Leave the house if you need to. All you can say to yourself at this point is, "The worst has happened, and it is over." Let the professionals take charge from there.

Review

Take a good look at the things you fear where your parents, your future, and their future are concerned.

Take concrete steps to help alleviate your fears. If your parents are sick, find out everything you can about their illnesses.

Take a course in CPR. You will feel less afraid of possible emergencies if you have prepared yourself for them.

Ask your parent about his or her fears. Find out what they think their future holds.

Ask your parents to make out living wills so their wishes will be known in case of emergency.

If you are afraid of nursing homes, look into some nursing homes to see if your fears are founded in fact.

Remember that the things we fear the most usually don't happen.

Don't think you have to brave it alone—call your local emergency number at the first sign of a problem.

7

GETTING AROUND

One evening my cousin, her boyfriend, and I volunteered to stay with my grandma so both my aunt and my mother Grandma's primary caregivers—could go to a family wedding. My cousin and her boyfriend were both pastry freaks. Since they figured we'd be there for quite a while, they brought a fabulous variety of sweets. We put on a pot of coffee, ate ourselves silly, and talked and laughed for hours. Grandma sat with us for a while telling stories of her youth and her home in Ireland. We had a great time. It was a party. None of us, however, really stopped to think how it would be if we had to do this day in and day out.

Of all the practical matters involved with taking your parents into your home, the day-in and day-out aspect is the one that may become most troublesome to the family as a whole. There are many possible circumstances that may limit your freedom and ability to get out of the house. Some of them are easily handled, others not. By realizing that this may become a problem, and working on possible solutions before the problem exists, you can keep yourself from becoming totally housebound with your parent.

Why Must I Stay Home?

The two most likely reasons that your parent(s) will have for not wanting you to leave them are sickness and fear for their safety. Both are important to you and your parent. Even if your parent seems healthy, remember, fear can lead to sickness. Fear sometimes takes on the aspects of self-fulfilling prophecy.

Sickness

Many elderly people are frail or sick. They can no longer maneuver as they once did. Even if they are not bedridden, they may be limited enough so that they can't do the simplest tasks by themselves. If this is the case, they can't possibly be left home alone. In order to judge the degree of disability you will be dealing with, and therefore your ability to get out, spend some time realistically evaluating your parent's health, mobility, and ability to perform simple tasks.

Health Overview

Can my mother/father walk unaided?

Is he or she wheelchair bound?

If a wheelchair is necessary, can he or she get into and out of it unaided?

If one is wheelchair bound, are there ramps installed making it possible to get into and out of the house?

Can he or she go to the bathroom by himself or herself?

Can he or she get into and out of bed unaided?

Can he or she prepare simple meals?

Can he or she be trusted to turn off the burners on the stove if used?

If both your parents are involved, as mine were, is the healthier of the two able to help the other one perform the tasks the other can't?

Does my father or mother have any health problem that may make them unexpectedly weak or faint?

If there was a fire, is it possible for him or her to get out of the house unaided?

Does my mother/father suffer from memory impairment?

Could he or she tell someone the address if lost? The telephone number?

Could he or she remember the emergency number if needed?

The answers to these questions will tell you how much or how little you need to be concerned about your ability to get out of the house. If your parents are healthy and mobile, you will probably have no problem once they have become accustomed to your home.

At first my mother could do things for herself. The memory loss caused by the Alzheimer's disease seemed to have more to do with forgetting to pay bills and do other periodic tasks like that. Eventually, though, her memory became very bad. She wouldn't remember to eat or she would put food on to cook and forget about it. At this point, she could no longer be left alone for any reason. I was afraid she would hurt herself or burn down the house. The only good thing about the memory loss was that she seemed to forget that she smoked. At least I no longer had to worry about her forgetting a lit cigarette. (J.M.)

Very Mobile or Moderately Impaired

Some changes may need to be made in order to help your parents be as self-sufficient as possible. For example, if your parent has trouble finding food that is stored on a bottom shelf because he or she cannot bend down or kneel down to look for it, move the food. Rearrange your cabinets so that anything they might need or use is at eye level. This way they won't have to do much bending or stretching and you certainly don't want your 80-year-old father climbing a stepladder to get the cereal down every morning. Do the same with your refrigerator. You may also want to take the time to go through the entire house with your parents' limitations in mind and shift whatever you see that may cause a hardship or be a barrier for them. The more you arrange things for their convenience, the less you will have to do yourself.

If they have trouble taking a shower, get a bath seat. This will make them feel more secure. They won't have to stand and move around in a wet tub. If hoisting themselves up from the toilet is a problem—you don't realize how low a toilet really is until someone with arthritis gets stuck on one—get a riser for the toilet. These are simple molded-plastic donuts that are placed on the toilet. They considerably raise the level at which the person sits, making the distance they have to stand up much shorter. They're simple, they're inexpensive, and they work wonders for elderly people who are stiffening up.

If you have a microwave, try to teach your parents to use it if they don't already know how. If they are not memory impaired and seem to grasp the general principles of the microwave, such as no metal objects and excessive steam production, encourage them to heat things in the microwave instead of on the stove. Usually the worst thing they can do to something in a microwave is dehydrate it. They can't start the house on fire with it nor can they set their own clothes on fire with it. One very important note of caution, however, involves pacemakers. If your parent wears a pacemaker, discourage any use of the microwave and make certain he or she is nowhere near the microwave when it is in use. Microwaves may disrupt the proper functioning of a pacemaker. Here are some examples of dependence and independence:

She can be left alone. If she's not feeling good she wants someone with her. But if she's feeling okay she can be left alone. If she is forewarned that we are going out for several hours, she will want to go somewhere there are people, like to my sister's. (S.L.)

My father is self-sufficient. He takes care of his own needs. He drives so he takes himself to the doctor and anywhere else he wants to go. He is healthy and more than capable of fixing his own food should he want to. I try not to take advantage of him by asking him to baby-sit too often, but he does do that too if the need arises. We are certainly not limited in our movements because he is there. Quite the contrary. We are probably able to do things that we wouldn't if he weren't here. (K.H.)

I did all the cooking. She would, on rare occasions, make her own lunch or a cup of tea, but she really didn't do much for herself. She was capable of doing more, though. (V.T.)

My mother was physically capable of being left alone. However, emotionally she could not tolerate being alone for two seconds. Going out without her for my wife and me was out of the question, as far as my mother was concerned. We took her just about every place we went. Whenever we left her alone with the kids, all of whom were at least in high school at the time and able to handle any emergency she might have, she would panic and call an ambulance. On more than one occasion, we came home from an evening out to find that Ma had gone to the hospital. Needless to say, this did cause problems. One of my sisters had to be there if we wanted to go out. Although they were more than willing to stay with Ma so we could go out, it did take all the spontaneity out of our lives. All evenings out or weekends away had to be planned enough in advance to make sure one of my sisters was available. (P.M.)

Severely Impaired and Bedridden

In both of these cases, you will probably find yourself homebound unless you take definite steps to avoid it. Leaving a severely impaired or bedridden person alone even for a short while is very dangerous and at the very least will cause terrible anxiety for the elderly person involved. In this case, it will be necessary to review your life-style rather than your parent's in order to determine what steps should be taken to ease the overall effect this will have on your life.

If you were very active before your parent moved in and suddenly find yourself homebound, you will become resentful and overwhelmed. This can lead to depression which will be of no help to either you or your parent. You can avoid becoming homebound by acknowledging the fact that it can happen and by taking some simple steps. First decide how often you need to get out to avoid feeling like a prisoner. Usually this isn't really a great amount of time and can be covered fairly easily. Here are some questions to help with a survey of your life-style:

What regular activities or chores take me out of the house during the day?

What social activities am I involved in during the day on a regular basis?

What activities are my children involved in that take me out of the house?

How often do my partner and I go out to socialize with friends?

Are my partner and I in the habit of going out to dinner often?

Do we often go away for weekends with friends or with the children?

How much time do I feel I need on a daily or weekly basis to myself with no outside interruptions?

Which of the above activities can I give up without feeling deprived or resentful?

Which of the above activities am I not willing to give up?

When you finish this survey of your activities, you will have a fairly clear idea of how much time you are going to need help with. This will differ greatly from person to person. Some people are not terribly social and enjoy spending the majority of their time at home. They may not feel overly restricted in taking care of a seriously debilitated parent. Others, however, are very social and will become very frustrated and resentful if they suddenly find themselves completely tied to the house. Most people are somewhere in between. They won't mind staying put most of the time, but do have a need to socialize or just to get out by themselves once in a while.

Don't depend on your love for your seriously debilitated parent carrying you through an extended period of isolation. Love alone isn't enough. You will need breaks and should pre-plan them. Where can you get help? There are many alternatives. Home-nursing agencies can be of help. If the agency is large enough, they can probably provide someone for short periods, or even to let you take a weekend getaway. You do not necessarily have to hire someone on a daily basis. Do you have brothers and sisters who live in your area? Keeping your parents company while you go out or go away is a very good way for them to do their share in helping your parents. Have your brothers and sisters take turns staying on a regular basis so that you and your husband or you and your kids can get out as a family to do something fun and relaxing. Watching a sick parent deteriorate daily puts a heavy strain on you and your family. You will need all the relaxation and fun you can get. If not bedridden, Adult Day Care is an excellent choice.

Do your parents have healthy brothers and sisters? Ask them for help. They will probably be glad to come and visit with their brother or sister while you go out. Check your local hospitals and nursing homes. Many of them now offer a service generally termed "respite care." This simply means that they are aware that full-time caregivers need a break from time to time. They have set aside space in the nursing home or hospital and for a fee will care for your loved one while you go on vacation. Keep this in mind. If your parent is very debilitated, it may be the only way you can arrange to get away and be totally confident that your parent is being properly cared for.

Anxiety Attacks

Anxiety attacks are a little harder to deal with than an obviously debilitated state. The older and more frail a person gets, the more likely he or she is to suffer from anxiety attacks. For example:

My mother's entire life could be described with some degree of accuracy as an anxiety attack. (P.M.)

My mother has anxiety attacks. They gave her a mild tranquilizer. It seems to help. (S.L.)

My mother was on so many medications that it was sometimes hard to tell whether she was reacting to medication or she was having physical problems. She complained to the doctor about being anxious all of the time. I think he was afraid to prescribe a sedative so he gave her a placebo. It worked, or at least she said it worked and that's what counts. (V.T.)

You may find that your parents don't want you to leave them alone simply because they are afraid. They may not even be sure what they are afraid of, or even that they are afraid. They may only know that they panic if you are gone. This happened in our case. My mother panicked every time I left the house. It made no difference that there were other adults there. I was the only one she felt could help her. This, of course, was not true, but it was a very real problem for her and became a real problem for me. In her case, an anxiety attack could bring on a breathing attack. She knew this but wasn't able to control it. It took time and much patience on everyone's part to get her to trust other people enough to stay calm when I wasn't there.

If you should encounter this problem, slowly start turning over some of the things you do for your parent to other people. Little by little, as your parents see that nothing drastic happens to them while other people are tending to their needs, they will relax a little. It took about two weeks with a nurse's aide before my mother relaxed enough for me to leave her with the aide.

Signs of Anxiety Attacks

Chances are your parent is not going to just come out and say, "I panic when you're not here, so you can't leave." Anxiety takes much subtler approaches. For example, I often meet a friend of mine for breakfast. We have done this for years. I would announce a day or two beforehand that I was meeting her for breakfast as was my habit. Each time, however, my mother would take a turn for the worse on the morning I had planned to go out. I would then have to call my friend and tell her I couldn't meet her.

It took three or four of these episodes before I started to figure out what was going on. My mother was not consciously doing this. She did, in fact, have trouble breathing on those mornings. She probably would have been very hurt if I had suggested that she just didn't want me to go out. The solution was simple. The next time we planned to meet for breakfast, I didn't tell my mother I was going out. I was out and back before she even woke up. There were, of course, other people in the house with her. She was not alone and was in no danger. She just didn't trust them enough to be comfortable with me gone.

Our overall solution to the problem of anxiety attacks keeping us in the house was to slowly build a list of people Mom did feel safe with. This had to be done through trial and error because even she didn't know who she was going to feel safe with. Eventually, we had a long enough list that we could get out of the house without worrying that she would have an attack simply because we were gone.

It takes time and patience to combat anxiety and fear. It can be done, though, and is essential to your well-being and that of your family as a whole.

My mother seemed to become anxious about everything. There were no physical reasons that I was aware of that prevented her from being left alone, but every time we went out, something would go wrong. Somebody would be sneaking about the house. The furnace would make strange noises. The dog would act funny and scare her. None of these things would happen if we were there. (K.V.)

Leading a Normal Life

Your life will definitely change when you take in your parents. You are adding people to your household. But the change needn't be for the worse. The key is not to stand on your own two feet. Enlist the help of as many different people as you can. Your activity level will probably increase, but this can be pleasurable and introduce you to a whole new group of friends. It can also strengthen your relationship with your extended family members. Your life can be normal or it can't be—it depends on what you do to deal with the situation.

I think we're living a normal life. In fact, it's probably extraordinary. I have a full-time job with a lot of responsibility and I have a lot of responsibility at home. I think that's normal. I think my father's being with us as one of the family is normal also. I think a lot of people are doing this sort of thing. (K.H.)

I don't think our life is normal. Not certainly what it would be with just me and my husband and the kids. This has definitely disrupted our lives. She really doesn't want to be left alone. No. Even if she's feeling good, I have to remember, oh, Mom has to have breakfast, or Mom has to have lunch at one, or Mom has to have dinner at six. I don't let my kids go further than I can see and sometimes that means putting Ma's intercom in the front window so I can hear her and watch the kids. That's not normal. (S.L.)

I realized before my mother moved into my home that she was beset by emotional difficulties, and could hardly expect that life with Ma was going to be perfectly normal. (P.M.)

Fighting Your Parents' Isolation
Unless you live very close (within a block or two) of your parents' former home, they will not be able to see their friends and neighbors as often as they used to. Try not to let your parents become isolated and totally dependent on you for entertainment. Have them invite the neighbors they were close to to your home. Encourage them to go back to the old neighborhood to visit with old friends. If they can no longer drive, offer to take them and pick them up. It will be a break for you and they won't feel that the life that they were used to is totally over.

Encourage your parents, if they are healthy enough, to join a local senior-citizens group and meet new friends. Senior-citizen centers usually offer a variety of activities and can sometimes provide transportation for those elderly who cannot drive. Many senior centers also offer day-care programs for seniors who have impairments. These programs work very well for seniors who live with children who work full-time. Some day-care programs combine senior day-care and child day-care. Many seniors enjoy the chance to be around children. They find it relaxing and fun.

If you have both of your parents and one is too debilitated to visit with old friends or join a seniors group, try to encourage the healthy parent to continue to be socially active. The isolation and depression that can come as a result of being confined to the house can cause illness. One sick parent is more than enough to cope with. Try to keep the other one healthy by encouraging him or her to be active.

New Activities

Even if your parent is physically debilitated, he or she will still need entertainment and distraction from his or her physical problems. Try to find activities that can be done at home that are fun and diverting.

Many elderly people enjoy playing board games. Your parents may not even be aware of some of the board games that are available. Unfortunately, as our children grow older we become less and less likely to check out the new toys and games on the market. A new-found interest in toys and games can be fun for the whole family. For example, my mother had never played Trivial Pursuit until she moved in with us. She did not have to be physically active to play this game, and since we always played partners, her partner would read the questions. Her mind was clear and sharp and she thoroughly enjoyed the game and the interaction with other people. There are many such games on the market. Do some exploring in your local toy store. Your whole family will probably be pleasantly surprised.

Help Is the Answer

You will be of no help to your parents if you become overwhelmed, angry, and resentful. Get help. You can lead a normal life even with very frail parents if you don't let your pride get in the way. Too often the attitude expressed by the phrase, "No problem, I can handle it," leads to an overstressed, overwrought person seeing only the problems and never getting a chance to experience the good things. Don't let this happen to you.

I joined an Alzheimer's support group. This was made up of family members of Alzheimer's patients. They completely understood what I was going through. In addition to getting welcome support, I made many new friends. Although they held weekly meetings, it often wasn't possible for me to get to the meetings because I couldn't leave my mother alone. They gave me their phone numbers and encouraged me to call. This I could do. Just hearing a friendly, understanding voice on the other end of the phone was a relief. (J.M.)

I already belonged to AA when my mother came to live with us. I tried to get her to join Al-Anon but she would have no part of it. I eventually joined Adult Children of Alcoholics (ACOA) and went both to AA and ACOA meetings. The support I got at these meetings was essential for my health and well-being. They helped me to understand that my mother was emotionally overwhelmed after spending so many years with a practicing alcoholic. The people at the meetings helped me to remember that my health and sanity were valuable things and often kept me from feeling resentful and put-upon. The Serenity Prayer [God grant me the serenity to accept the things I cannot change, the courage to change the things I can, and the wisdom to know the difference], used in both these groups for spiritual help, became my daily help. When I'd start to become frustrated, I would silently repeat the prayer and it never failed to help me through the tough time. (K.V.)

You Are Just as Important as Your Parents
You cannot always put your needs and desires in the background waiting for some future date when your responsibilities are no longer so heavy. What you are really doing in that case is saying, "As soon as they die, I will be able to live again." You don't want this. It leads to guilt. Guilt adds to

stress and only makes the situation worse. Take care of yourself. Keep your health strong. Work an exercise program into your week's activities. Exercise is an excellent stress reducer. Be sure to eat right and get enough rest while you can. If the time comes when your parent can't get through the night, you are going to need the reserve strength and energy that being healthy and in good shape will give you.

You Are Just as Important as Your Brothers and Sisters

Get your whole family involved. Don't let your brothers and sisters beg off taking their share of the responsibility and work. It isn't good for them and it isn't good for you. More than one family has suffered as a whole because one child assumed all the responsibility of taking care of aging parents and then resented the brothers and sisters for not helping. Don't let it happen. Tell them when you need help and just exactly what kind of help you need. By doing these things, you can enjoy the experience with your parents and live a different but still normal life.

> All of my sisters have gone to heroic lengths to help my mother. My mother's problems were always considered family problems. Even when my mother lived in my home, my sisters never ceased to be supportive. (P.M.)

> Everybody helped. Everybody took turns. We all tried to make her happy. Our mom's problems were considered family problems. We all tried. (V.T.)

> After one of my mother's surgeries, she went to my sister's to recuperate. My brother stops in at least once and usually twice a week. He takes care of the Medicare for her. Yes, my brother and sisters all help. It is considered a family situation. They don't expect me to do everything without help. (S.L.)

Review

Evaluate your parents' health to decide if and when they can be left alone.

Reorganize the house to make it easier for your parents to do things for themselves.

Get bathroom equipment (bath seat, toilet riser) that will help them help themselves.

Review your own life-style to see how much outside activity you will need and how much you can do without.

Do not depend on your love for your parents to carry you through alone—get help.

Determine whether your parent is suffering from panic attacks.

Build a list of people who your parent trusts enough to be left with.

Do not become isolated.

Try not to let your parent become isolated.

Find recreational activities that can be done at home with a sick parent.

Exercise to reduce stress.

Remember, you are just as important as your parent and your brothers and sisters.

8

LIVING TOGETHER HAPPILY

When you begin this new journey with your parents, you may be apprehensive because of past memories. Much of your relationship with your parents revolved around their expectations for you as you grew up. They told you what you were expected to do and punished you if you didn't do it. You probably had a certain amount of fear concerning your parents when you were small. They were bigger than you and could force you to do as they wanted. As you grew and matured, you were still expected to do certain things in certain ways. They were the bosses.

Now you are about to live with your parents again, but the relationship is going to be totally different. How is it going to be different? Different can be better or it can be worse. We found, through our experience, that this can be a time of discovery and of great happiness.

Discovery

As you are growing up, you take very little time to consider your parents as actual people. They have just always been there. They don't have a past. They were never children. Now is the time that you can find your parents as the people they are. Often the phrase, "When I was your age," brings shivers and the urge to run. In the past, this phrase often preceded a lecture about what we were doing wrong. It needn't be that way now. Encourage your parents to relive their pasts. Ask them to tell you about their lives when they were young children. You may find that you really didn't know your parents at all.

The Family History
Use this found time with your parents to learn the history of the family. Find out about your grandparents. Many of us know the basic facts about our families, but don't know why many things were done. If your grandparents came from a different country, ask your parents why they felt the need to leave their homeland. See if they know the story of your grandparents' journey, the hardships they faced, the discoveries they made. My children found the story of my grandmother's emigration from Ireland to this country very interesting. Through my mother's retelling of her mother's life, they grew to know a woman they had never met. Shortly before my parents came to stay with us, my sister had occasion to go to Ireland and visit the birthplace of our grandfather. She was able to add updated information about the family to my mother's recollections.

We also all found out that our father was very involved in sports as a young man, even though we really didn't remember him being very athletic as we grew up. He told us of a time that he ran for public office before we were born. These are all things the family found very interesting.

Because my parents were living with us, my aunts and uncles came often to visit them. We are all adults now, so many of the faces parents put on for their kids have been dropped. They told stories of their young adult years and the kinds of jams they got into. We began to see our parents more as people than as parents. The role of parent had disappeared. These were just two people who had experienced much in their lives. They had lived through the Depression and struggled to help their parents keep their homes and put bread on the table. They had lived through World War II and all the disruptions and heartaches that brought. They were young before all of the wonder drugs we take for granted today were discovered. They saw friends and family members die of diseases that hardly anyone dies of today.

Many of these subjects just had never come up before. There wasn't time for them to come up before when they were busy being "parents." Had they remained in their own home, these subjects may never have come up. We are all busy. We visit or go to our parents' house to help them around the house and we're gone again. We all get together on the holidays and spend the time talking about news or the holiday itself. It is in the quiet of a normal evening at home that the real stories of the past begin to emerge. The evenings when all the work is done and everyone's just sitting around relaxing. This is when your parents will emerge as people you want to get to know.

> One night I asked my mother what had attracted her to my father. I really, at this point, didn't remember too many good things about him. She started talking about when she was young. She said she loved to dance and go to parties. She said she even had secret dreams of becoming a dancer. She said Dad was the best-looking guy in the neighborhood, but even more important than that, she said he danced like a dream. She told stories of going to supper clubs with Dad and dancing the night away. She talked of the big bands and how fun they were to dance to. Suddenly I could picture them, looking elegant, with my dad whirling Mom around the dance floor—young and in love. I had never thought of them that way before. (K.V.)

Self-Discovery

For better or for worse, you will probably find out a lot about yourself through this experience with your parents.

We all have a tendency to feel that we are unique, and we are. We may, however, not be quite as unique as we think we are. You may find yourself mirrored in your mother and father. Habits and thinking patterns that you have developed over the years may have had their origin in your parents. You may not be aware of this until your parents come to live with you. You may also find it disconcerting at first. I found a lot of my mother in me. The similarities often caused tension between us. I, like most people, didn't really think I was at all like my mother. I am actually quite like my mother.

Use this time to find the roots of some of the things that bother you. Do you have fears that just always seemed to be there? Ask your parents what kinds of things they were afraid of. Especially ask you mother. Since in the years you were being raised, mothers generally spent more time with the kids than fathers did, you are more likely to have picked up her fears than his. Is she afraid of driving on the highway? Are you? Is she afraid to live alone? Are you?

Everyone has different fears. Most people have at least a few fears that have always puzzled them. If you were ever in a car accident, it is not hard to understand why you might be afraid of cars. If, on the other hand, you were never involved in an accident and you have a fear of traveling in cars, you may be just as puzzled as everyone else about why you have this fear. This example comes to mind because of an experience with my mother after she moved in with us. I do, at times, experience small to medium panic attacks while riding in cars. I've never been in a serious accident, and could not understand why I would become so afraid in a car. Then one day, I was taking my mother to the doctor. She insisted on sitting in the back seat even though it was only the two of us. She said she felt safer in the back. As soon as I pulled away from the curb, she took out her rosary and prayed furiously until we reached our destination. Then I remembered that the whole time we were growing up, she would sit in the back seat and say the rosary until we safely got where we were going. Her sister was killed in a traffic accident. My brother fell out of a car when he was a baby, although he was not injured. It took this experience with my mother to show me where my fear was coming from. She had inadvertently taught us to be afraid by her reactions to cars while we were growing up. My own fear of cars has diminished greatly since this incident. Knowing where it came from has helped me to fight it.

This is just one simple example of the kinds of things you can learn about yourself from observing your parents. There are many, many more. Be alert. Use this time to learn and to appreciate. You can emerge with a relationship you never dreamed could happen.

Building an Adult-to-Adult Relationship

Probably one of the first shocks to your nervous system after you move your parents in is that you may find yourself feeling like a kid again. Almost certainly not feeling like a kid in the sense that you have the vim and vigor of a 10-year-old. (That would be nice.) The feeling that I mean is that tendency you have as a kid to expect your parents to review your work or your actions and give their comments, critical or otherwise, on what you are doing. After all, they probably did feel the right, if not the duty, to let you know what you were doing wrong for the entire time you lived with them.

Quite often, that feeling of expectation of criticism comes back directly after your parents move in. This may only be in your mind and your parents may never have considered telling you how to do things in your own home. However, sometimes, they too fall back into the old pattern of thinking that it's their duty to tell you how something should be done. Regardless of whether it is in your mind, or is actually happening, this situation can cause trouble and resentment. It is best for all involved that you put a stop to it as soon as possible. But how? There are several things you can do.

Real or Imagined. The first thing you should do is determine whether your parents are really treating you like a child, or if you just feel they are. You might want to ask yourself some questions:

What exactly has my parent said or done that makes me feel they are treating me like a child? List specific examples.

What were the circumstances surrounding these situations? For example, was I having difficulty doing something and my parent stepped in and explained how he or she thought it could be done?

What tone of voice was used in these instances?

Do most of the instances listed concern fairly neutral topics, or do they concern my relationships with my partner and children?

Is it possible that my parent was simply mentioning alternative solutions to these situations?

Are there any circumstances under which I would appreciate my parents' observations? If so, what are they?

On what subjects are my parents likely to have more expertise than me or my spouse?

Do I have a defensive attitude concerning suggestions offered by my parent?

You may find, after answering these questions, that you are being hypersensitive to your parents. This is not unusual at the outset of this type of living arrangement. You are not sure how it is going to work out, your parents are not sure how it is going to work out, and everyone involved probably wants it to work out well. This can cause everyone to be hypersensitive for a while. If this is the case, problems will probably start correcting themselves without too much effort on anyone's part as you all become more used to the situation.

Sometimes, though, the hypersensitivity continues to worsen until the tension in the home is unbearable. This situation cannot be tolerated and often cannot be corrected by the people living in the home without outside help. Be honest in your evaluations if you can. If possible, talk to a counselor who specializes in the problems of the elderly and of the caregivers of the elderly. The senior-support services of your local hospital should be able to help you find such a counselor.

If you don't feel comfortable talking to a stranger, arrange time to meet and talk to a trusted friend. Set your meeting in a neutral place where you can relax and tell your friend what is going on at home. Often, just voicing your frustrations will help ease the tension. You may feel disloyal and guilty at first if you are complaining about your parents, but try to keep in mind that no one is perfect.

Many of us grew up with families such as the Cleavers from "Leave It to Beaver," the Stones from "The Donna Reed Show," or even the Bradys from "The Brady Bunch" as our only models of what other families were like. Keep in mind that all families fall short of the examples set by these families. Very few mothers look and sound calm and perfect all the time. We can't let unrealistic ghosts from the past haunt our relationships today. These mothers never went to a friend to complain about their families because the writers of the shows wouldn't let them. The writers gave them near-perfect families. Unfortunately, we don't have writers putting words in our mouths or the mouths of our family members. We have to improvise life. This can make the whole business of living very untidy.

Normal people become frustrated and need to vent their feelings. If that means bending a friend's ear about your frustrations concerning your parents, bend away. A good friend will understand that you love your parents even if they do frustrate you at times. Your friend will not think less of you or your parents.

Parent Abuse

Getting help with your frustrations and anger is of vital importance. The incidence of physical abuse of the elderly is increasing at an alarming rate. In some cases of elderly abuse, the children are playing out the model they were taught as young children. Abusive homes breed abusive people who go on to establish abusive homes.

In some cases, however, explosive and potentially harmful situations are set up by well-meaning people who become emotionally and physically overwhelmed and who don't know how to escape. With help from friends, caregiver support groups, and counselors, you can escape an emotionally explosive situation without having to escape from your home.

An example of this type of explosive situation that I will probably never forget came up while I was doing some research for this book. I was at the library checking out an inordinate number of books about the care of the elderly. The librarian, a woman in her fifties named Mary, asked about the books. I mentioned I was working on a book about caring for elderly parents and some of the problems that can arise. To my surprise and her dismay, tears welled up in Mary's eyes and within seconds, she was sobbing. She struggled valiantly but couldn't seem to stop. In an effort to save face, she dashed into the back room. I followed her.

When she had recovered enough to talk, she said she was an only child who was caring for her elderly mother. Since she was the sole support of both of them, she had to work. It frightened her to leave her mother home alone during the day, but she couldn't afford to hire help. She saw her mother as unreasonably demanding and spent every evening from the time she got home from work listening to her mother's complaints and doing an endless list of jobs her mother wanted done. Mary was a physical and emotional wreck. She said she was terribly ashamed because although she saw herself as a caring person, she had at times screamed at her mother to leave her alone and on at least one occasion had told her mother she wished she were dead. Mary was terrified that she was becoming a monster.

Mary hadn't been out of the house for anything other than work and grocery shopping in months. Going out to enjoy herself was out of the question. Mary and her mother had death grips on each other. They were both suffering terribly.

Mary was like many people involved in taking care of elderly parents. They tell themselves, "They're my parent, so they're my problem. I'll just have to cope." They don't seem to realize they are trying to do single-handedly what it takes three full shifts of nurses to do in a hospital—give someone around-the-clock care. It really can't be done without destroying both the parent and the sole caregiver.

Both Mary and her mother were in a very dangerous situation. Mary was reaching her breaking point. She had already started reacting with a certain amount of verbal abuse. The fact that she felt shame and remorse did not mean she wouldn't continue the verbal abuse, it simply meant that emotionally she was even more burdened—this time not by her mother's actions but by her own. There is a very thin line between verbal abuse and physical abuse. It can be crossed in an unguarded second. The potential for irreparable damage in Mary's situation was tremendous.

Mary was an intelligent woman, but she had fallen into the trap of thinking that asking for help was a sign of weakness. She said she really hadn't told anyone how tired, frustrated, and angry she was because she felt guilty talking about her mother. She thanked me profusely for talking with her. I hadn't talked with her. Except for giving her the number of a senior-support service, I really hadn't said much of anything. Mary did all the talking. She had helped herself by getting her feelings out and talking about them.

When I brought the books back, I saw Mary again. She had called the senior-support number and had been referred to a caregiver-support group. The situation at home had not changed miraculously over night, but it was changing. Mary had actually gone out to dinner and a show while one of the support group members stayed with her mother. The last time I talked to her, she was trying to get up the nerve to suggest an adult day-care program to her mother. She hoped her mother would be more pleasant to deal with if she got involved with other people. Although Mary's physical situation hadn't changed drastically, her attitude had. She now knew she had options and didn't have to carry the load alone.

Mary and her mother both could have ended up sick or hurt if things hadn't changed. It is this totally isolated, potentially dangerous situation that you should avoid at all cost. It would be much better for the elderly person involved to be placed in a nursing home than to stay in a situation in which desperation and fatigue breeds abuse.

You're Not So Dumb After All

Quite often, elderly people feel that they are no longer needed and that people don't feel that they are good for anything. This can be especially true of an aging parent who is no longer healthy and vigorous. Now that they are again involved actively in a growing family situation, they may try to prove that they can be useful. Sometimes this makes them try too hard and appear pushy.

If you recognize and acknowledge your parents' need to be useful, this problem will often solve itself. No matter who you are, or how accomplished you are, there must be things that your parent knows about and is accomplished in that you are not. It is surprising how seemingly insignificant these things can seem to you, but they can be very important to your parent. A few personal examples may help to illustrate this:

My mother's kitchen was very small with little storage space. In addition to this, she had difficulty seeing. As a result, she had organized that kitchen down to the last egg noodle. She didn't have to look to tell you where anything was. My kitchen on the other hand is large and has plenty of storage space. I have no difficulty seeing. My point here is, my kitchen is basically very disorganized. I really don't have too much trouble finding things, but things have been known to disappear into the drawers and cabinets never to be seen again. My mother and I would no sooner sit down in the kitchen to have a cup of coffee and she would start on my disorganization. My pots were in the wrong place, my canned goods should be in a different cabinet, and the first time I opened the bottom pots-too-big-to-fit-anywhere-reasonably cabinet in her presence and a pile of lids fell out, well this was something that could never have happened in her house. She was right. She was much better organized than I was. She had to be. She couldn't see to find things.

This same type of go-around happened with distressing regularity when she first moved in. I felt that she was being overly critical and became very nervous about doing anything around the house, especially in the kitchen. I solved the problem by washing the walls.

Yes, I did say washing the walls. Over the years, I have developed the habit of attacking the walls when I have a problem that is upsetting me, and which I am having difficulty solving. Usually the wall-washing binges start sometime in the middle of the night. I have a problem, I can't sleep, I get frustrated, I get up and wash a wall. My family had become very used to this over the years. If my kids got up for school in the morning and found me washing walls, they stayed out of my way until I put the buckets away. They knew something was wrong and didn't want any backlash. My mother, however, had never witnessed this since it was a habit I developed after I moved out of her house.

About two months after my parents moved in, my mother woke up in the middle of the night and heard a noise in the dining room. She got up to investigate. What she found was her youngest daughter furiously scrubbing the dining-room walls. It was about 3:00 in the morning. Needless to say, she thought I had slipped a cog. It did get her curious enough to ask what was going on. So, at 3:30 that memorable morning, my mother and I sat down and probably had the best, most open discussion we had ever had in our entire lives.

I explained to her how I was feeling more and more inadequate because I couldn't seem to do anything as well as she thought I could. She was horrified to hear this. It had never been her intention to make me feel that I couldn't do anything right. She knew that super organization had helped her and thought she was doing me a favor by pointing out the problems in my organizational strategies. She also told me that she was impressed by the way I managed to run the house, work full-time, and still have time to help her and my dad. I never realized that she thought this way. We became more than mother and daughter that night, we became friends.

What Can They Help You With?

After this talk with my mother, we reorganized the kitchen. She was good. She made suggestions about the pots and pans and how the staples could be better organized. We found new places for some of the things in my kitchen that had been irritating me for years. This also led to my mother planning the menus for us. She couldn't stand at the stove and cook, but she could give me suggestions and she could, when she was feeling well, peel potatoes and do other small tasks like that. We had many good discussions while we worked together in the kitchen.

Ask your parents what they would like to do around your house. Maybe your father enjoys lawn work and would like to help keep the garden or lawn. Perhaps your mother would love to pass on her special recipes to you or show you how to do something you don't know how to do. My mother hated slipcovers so she had taught herself how to reupholster furniture. She showed me how to do it. I will probably never use this skill as I do not find sewing in general as fun and relaxing as she did, but we had fun working on some of my furniture together. She also taught my daughter how to sew. My daughter still sews when she has the time and enjoys it.

The possibilities for your parent to be helpful around your home are endless. As I have said before, don't think for them. Don't assume that because you are extremely busy and would love the chance to do nothing for a while that they feel the same way. There is a good possibility that they have been doing too little for too long and would relish the chance to get involved. Kathy's (K.H.) father does all the food shopping for the family. Since he is not rushed, he has the time and the patience to shop for the best sales. Kathy is the first to admit that her father is a much better shopper than she is. These are just a few examples of how you and your parents can combine your skills to form a happily functioning family. Try it. Everyone will probably like it.

We're All Just People

We grow up doing what our parents tell us to do. Most of us break out of that mold by moving away and starting life on our own, whether we marry or not. We make our own decisions, and our own mistakes. It is up to us if we want to tell our parents what is going on in our lives. Chances are, you tell your parents about your successes and forget to mention the mistakes you made getting there. That's okay. As adults, we have a right to tell what we want and keep the rest to ourselves.

When we move our parents into our homes, we are put in a strange position. We are adults, yes. We have as many successes and failures as we did when we lived apart. The difference is, they are now there to see the mistakes. They are no longer getting the edited version of our lives. They're seeing the live, unrehearsed performance. This can make us nervous at the beginning.

If your parent seems to want to become actively involved in your family's life (and not all do), find a happy medium. Recognize the fact that life and experience do count and that they probably do know more than you give them credit for.

I'm reminded of something Mark Twain said: "When I was 17, I thought my father was stupid. When I was 21, I was amazed at how much the old man had learned in 4 years." I always knew that my father was bright, and a very good mathematician. I guess I have come to the realization that had circumstances been different, he would have had a much different life. By that I mean he was college-bound, intending to be a lawyer when the war [WWII] broke out. And so he was in the army and when he came out, he went into a trade. That was fine. It was a good trade and lucrative for him. I know though that my father is intelligent enough, has enough natural intelligence, to have made an excellent attorney and an even better CPA. (K.H.)

Ask your parents' opinions, but make it clear that you do not feel bound to accept their opinions and act on them. Let them know how you feel and reassure them that even if you don't act on a suggestion of theirs that you do appreciate their opinions and that you do consider them valid and helpful.

The parent/child relationship can get very strained in adolescence; it can stay that way until the day you leave your parents' house. Be sure you don't pick up where you left off if that was the case. Act with confidence in matters concerning your family and your life and your parents will soon see that you are more than capable of living your own life.

Enjoying the Extended Family

Although living in family groups in an extended family was once fairly common, things have changed. Most families live only with their immediate family group—mother, father, children. The increased mobility brought about by the car and the airplane made the decision to move away from the concentrated family an easier decision to make. You can get almost anywhere in the continental United States in just a matter of hours. Today when people move away from their families, it does not necessarily mean that they will never see them again as it often did in the past. Modern families get used to grandparents living across the country and visiting once or twice a year. Aunts and uncles may be people that your children rarely, if ever, see. Where once people were used to staying in the same neighborhood for most of their lives, and having the majority of the relatives living within a radius of a few miles, this has become a thing of the past.

The opportunity to have your parents living in your home can open a whole new world to you and your children. My children were fascinated by the things that my parents had never seen or done. So many things we take for granted were out of reach for our parents. It is good for your children to start to see things through the eyes of the past generations. Customs that were common in our parents' time, or our grandparents' time, that have gone out of practice can be the subjects of many enjoyable conversations.

Because my parents were living with us, many relatives who commonly visited them, but not us, started coming to our house to visit them. Great aunts and uncles that the kids had seen at family gatherings but really didn't know became in their minds part of the family. We came to enjoy and look forward to these visits as much as my parents did. I really hadn't been aware of all that I was missing until these people were reintroduced on a personal basis. We have, since my mother's death, kept up with the visits. None of us are willing, at this point, to go back to the old way of seeing each other at weddings and funerals only. I now make weekly calls to aunts and uncles whom I rarely had occasion to think about let alone call before my parents moved in with us.

Most of all an extension of family means an extension of love, and love is something we all need as much of as we can get. When my mother's health took a drastic turn for the worse and she became bedridden, I don't think we would have been able to cope with it had it not been for my wonderful aunts and uncles who came to our aid. They gave unselfishly of their time and their affection. They made it possible for me to get uninterrupted sleep. They made it possible for me to see a purpose in all that was happening. In the end, on the day my mother passed away, they were there to help us and to help her. She knew they were there and that they loved her. She knew that they would help my family and those of my brother and sister to get through this time. They helped her to find peace.

Although dealing with my mother's illness was stressful both physically and emotionally, I would not hesitate to do it again. The gifts that we received—stronger family ties, the realization that we are not alone in our problems, and the knowledge that people want to help—far outstripped any problems that we encountered. This sentiment was basically repeated by everyone I talked to while working on this book. There were irritations, certainly. For some there were major health or psychological problems. Everyone agreed, though, that there was also much happiness, much learning, and much growing that took place in their lives as a result of this experience. All were thankful that they had accepted the challenge of forming a new and extended family.

Review

Learn to know your parents as people instead of "parents."

Use this time to find out more about their backgrounds, their parents, their upbringing.

Use this time to find out what attitudes and/or fears you may have picked up from your parents.

Acknowledge your parents' expertise. Encourage help in the areas they are more versed in than you.

Ask them what they would like to do to help with daily tasks and welcome that help.

Learn to deal with your parents on an adult/adult basis instead of the adult/child basis you were probably on when you left their house.

Enjoy the benefits of the extended family. Welcome family members into your home and your life.

Accept any help offered.

Look for the bright spots instead of dwelling on the hard times or problems.

9
Making The Decision

The decision to move from one house to another is always hard. The decision to combine two households can be twice as difficult to make. When I first asked my mother to consider moving into our home, she was absolutely set against it. It took three years for her to change her mind and make the move.

In our case, the reason behind the move was Mother's failing health. Although she and my father were getting by in their own home, it was more and more apparent that she was getting weaker and he was not going to be able to take care of her. Financially, their combined social security and his pension were enough to support them.

Asking my parents to move was a definite break in procedure. When my grandmother became too weak to be left alone due to minor strokes, my mother quit her job to take care of her. Since an unmarried aunt lived with Grandma, my mother and aunt split her care between them. Mom would go to Grandma's every morning so my aunt could go to work. My dad would pick Mom up after work and my aunt would take over. This routine completely disrupted my mother's life for six years and was very hard on my aunt as well because each of them was basically alone with Grandma all of the time. Since Grandma would pass out when she had these little strokes, she needed someone there constantly.

I'm not sure about my aunt, but I know my mother was terrified of medical emergencies. She was never sure she would be able to handle them. Although I didn't think about it at the time, I realize now that the strain on both of them must have been horrendous.

Although there is no actual way to connect the occurrences following my grandmother's death, it is a fact that my aunt died at the age of 53 within a few years of my grandmother's death and my mother fell prey to the disease that would plague her for 15 years and from which she finally died.

There is growing evidence that severe prolonged strain can indeed weaken our immune systems. I found myself in a position of wanting to help my mother, but not wanting to do it the way she had. I couldn't spend every day at her house. I needed to find a way to fit helping her into my daily routine as best I could. And I wanted all the help and support I could get. For me, that meant getting my family involved in the process.

When my mother was taking care of Grandma, we gave her no help with the exception of driving her and picking her up. Her days started at 6:00 and went to 6:00 or 7:00 at night. Then she would come home and make dinner. She should have shot the bunch of us, but she was a believer in standing on your own two feet. So, she took the responsibility and did more than she should have.

I'm not as selfless as my mother. I wanted help and I believe in asking for what I want. My mother suffered from chronic obstructive pulmonary disease (COPD). This condition severely limits breathing, and progresses slowly to the point where the victim cannot be physically active at all without discomfort. In addition to the chronic aspects of the disease, victims suffer acute attacks that cut off their breathing almost entirely and cause panic reactions. In the last three years of my mother's life, these attacks came more frequently and put her in a state of chronic anxiety.

The reasons for wanting my parents to come and live with my family seemed simple: she was sick and we could take care of her. No problem, right?

Wrong! Since I have yet to get the world to revolve to my tune, it took us three years and hundreds of hours of discussion before the deed was done. This is the case for many people. For others, there is no problem. For still others, the decision is made more by the parent than by the adult child. As witness the following examples:

At the time we suggested my mother move in, she was eager to do it. She had spent some time in a nursing home by this time and complained bitterly about the lack of attention, the food quality, and just about everything else. (P.M.)

The decision to move into our house was made by my father. He had always assumed that he would predecease my mother and he felt that when we moved into our house 10 years ago, we should be sure that there were sleeping arrangements on the first floor for my mother. She was an amputee and would need those kinds of accommodations. When, in fact, she died, he simply came and moved in. We didn't talk about it. He just said, "I'm going to let the lease go on the apartment," and he moved in. (K.H.)

My mother was the one who decided she would move in with us. She chose me. My sisters wanted her to move in with their families, but she chose to live here. I think it was because I was the last one to leave home. Six years ago when she first moved in, I had only been married three years. So I had lived with her up to three years before she moved in. I think she felt more used to me. Actually, she moved in twice. The first time was when my dad went into a nursing home. He had Alzheimer's disease. She didn't want to be alone. She had never lived alone. She was healthy then and it didn't change our lives much at all. She moved out shortly before our first child was born. She had been there a year and decided we needed the room and she needed to be on her own. I was not happy that she moved out because I didn't think it would work and it didn't. She moved back two years later. The day I came home from the hospital with our second child, my mother had surgery on her legs. She went to stay with my sister for a few weeks and then went back to her apartment, but from that point on, she didn't want the apartment. She was afraid to be alone. She was afraid something would happen and no one would be there for her. She moved back in with us. (S.L.)

I made the decision to bring my mother into our home. She wanted to come because she was in a nursing home. She didn't want to stay there but she also didn't want to live by herself. Unfortunately, she really didn't want to live with anybody else either. Where she wanted to live was in a hospital. That's the only place she was ever happy. (V.T.)

In our home, my husband was understanding and willing. The kids, all of whom are older, also took part in making this decision. The one phrase we wanted to avoid at all costs was, "No one asked me!" coming from a disgruntled partner, child, or young adult.

For Better or For Worse: Your Partner

My husband's willingness was partly due to the fact that his own mother had lived with us before she passed away. We both felt, and still do, that families should try to help each other. Here's another example:

My wife and I jointly made the decision to move my mother into our house. We discussed the matter at great length before the move. She was aware that my mother was a difficult person to care for. She was also aware that my three sisters had been shouldering all the responsibility for my mother up to this time and that I had been very skillfully side-stepping any of my responsibility. However, any guilt I may have felt for leaving my mother to my sisters was not enough to induce me to undertake my mother's care. I would not have considered it had not my wife expressed not only willingness, but eagerness to take on the job. My mother was a very unhappy person. She had many psychological problems and some physical ones that we were not fully aware of, but it made me and my wife sad that she should be so unhappy. If there was the slightest chance that we could make my mother's life happier, we both wanted to take the chance. (P.M.)

Prepare the Troops

Since you and your partner have probably never lived with each other's parents, some preparation will be necessary to acquaint each partner with the personalities he or she may have to deal with. If it is your parents who are moving in, your partner probably knows them only on a social basis. Since people have a tendency to be on their best behavior during social activities, your partner probably doesn't really know your parents. Of course, your parents are in the same position where your partner is concerned. All parties deserve to be prepared for the move. Does your father or your husband walk around the house in his underwear? Will this be a problem? Tell the person that this behavior might need to be changed. Does your hard-of-hearing mother blast the TV? Consider asking her to get a hearing aid. In any case, think about any idiosyncracies you and your husband have or your parents have and bring them up for discussion. For physical problems such as these, there is almost always a simple solution. Here are some rememberences of pre-moves:

Except for reminding her that the kids were not always quiet, there didn't seem to be too many things my mother really wanted to know. It was my wife and kids who I felt needed to be warned about my mother's peculiar habits. (P.M.)

My husband didn't mind my mother's moving in. He is very easygoing and he knew her well enough to know that she wouldn't interfere in our private lives. (S.L.)

My husband and I both wanted to help my mother. She had such a hard life with my father that we felt she deserved to be taken care of for once in her life. We did not, though, bother to explore the problems that her [previous] life with an active alcoholic might cause us. (K.V.)

Pre-move preparation can be accomplished in different ways. The way we found most helpful was to ask questions of each group about their concerns and to try to pinpoint any personality or behavior quirks that might be problematic. Although the questions below were initially directed at my husband, we found the same questions (with appropriate noun substitutions) very useful with my parents.

How Do You Really Feel?

How do you really feel about this move?

What is your most recurrent fear concerning the move?

Why are you consenting to the move?

Do you feel you need to know more about the in-law before the move?

How good or bad a relationship do you feel you have with your in-law?

Under what circumstances would you feel the living arrangements were not working out and should be terminated?

What do you feel is a reasonable amount of time for everyone to adjust?

Should you decide you do not like the living arrangements, what alternatives would you suggest?

Tell your spouse and your parents to be totally honest in their responses to these questions. Since you are emotionally attached to each of them, they may try to spare your feelings by glossing over areas that worry them. Be prepared to hear things you may not like. You, as the child of the parents who are moving in, hold a unique position in the matter. You love your partner and you love your parents. You may not see any reason they would not love each other. This may not be so. Your partner may feel your parents are dictatorial and interfering. Your parents may find your partner lacking in areas they feel are important. Have each person involved go over the questions privately with you. Try to remain objective and see all of the parties involved through the other person's eyes. Carefully consider how you will react if your parents and partner have difficulty getting along.

Before the move, have a meeting that includes you, your partner, and your parents. Since you will be the only one who knows what the concerns of each person were, try to gently lead the discussion in such a way that all stated concerns are addressed. It is not necessary to say who voiced a concern. It is only necessary to generally address the concerns so that each party will be forewarned and be able to give his or her opinion about possible problems and their solutions.

A 'Thank You' Is in Order

It is very easy to get caught up in the hectic physical activity involved with packing and moving. It is also very normal to be optimistic about the new arrangements. Under these circumstances, it is possible to forget to tell your partner how much you appreciate his or her willingness to rearrange the house and the family. We see a problem with our parents and feel moving them into our homes is the solution. This does not necessarily mean that our partners will see this as the best solution. If your partner agrees to the move, he or she is most likely doing it for you and not for your parents.

No matter how willing your partner appears, he or she will have some serious concerns about this change. You need, especially during the decision-making stage, to reassure your partner that you are aware of his or her feelings and that you are willing to keep an open mind as things progress. If not, your partner and the rest of your family can begin to feel trapped by circumstances.

'Family' Means Everybody

Involve your brothers and sisters in discussions of possible problems. Since everyone is different, they may be able to offer suggestions and insights that you are not aware of. My husband's sister, who had spent much time with their mother was very helpful in helping me understand my mother-in-law.

In addition to insights that may be offered by brothers and sisters, there is another very important reason to involve everyone. The person into whose home an elderly person moves should not, at any time, be considered wholly responsible for the parent if there are other siblings alive and well. I cannot stress this point too strongly. Many families have experienced serious damage because one person was expected to take on all of the care and problems of the parent.

I have three sisters. When Mom first moved in, they said they would help. They didn't, though. If I called and asked them to stay with her, their usual response was that she was just being a baby and didn't need anyone to stay with her. They would tell me not to take any nonsense from her. This was easy for them to say, but not so easy to accomplish. For whatever reason, she didn't want to be left alone and there were always problems when she was.

We also ran into a problem when my husband and I wanted to go on vacation. Every one of my sisters had what they considered a good reason why Mom couldn't stay with their families—not enough room, too much commotion for her, etc.

Anyway, the upshot of all this is that I got very, very resentful. They figured the problem of what to do with Mom was solved. I would take care of it. I came very close to telling them never to call or come to visit again. (K.V.)

This can and should be avoided at all costs. Even though one adult child may become the primary caregiver for an elderly parent, the other adult children need to be involved. This involvement can take. many forms. As Karen (K.V.) mentioned, sometimes people are needed to stay with the parent to give the primary caregiver an afternoon or evening off. Sometimes it helps for a sibling to take the parent into his or her home so the primary family can vacation or just get a little break.

If there are siblings involved who refuse to take any responsibility, there is a very good chance that your partner will become resentful. Why should he or she be expected to do for your parent what that parent's own children refuse to do?

The resentments caused by lack of help on the part of siblings can last a lifetime and destroy a family. Long after the parent has passed away, the feelings of being abandoned and taken advantage of by siblings can remain. Taking steps at the very beginning to avoid this situation can save your family from a lifetime of hard feelings and regrets.

Take Time to Consider

Some of the other considerations that should be dealt with by the adults are very physical in nature. What hours are you used to keeping? What hours are your parents used to keeping? Will they have a hard time getting used to people being up and around when they are trying to sleep? Will you have trouble if you are the early bird and they stay up late?

What about the kids? If your kids are older, do they have the same types of curfews you had as a teenager? Do you keep as close tabs on your adolescent children as your parents did on you? If not, will your parents be inclined to mention this to you?

Your parents probably did run a stricter home than you do. They did most of their child rearing before the day of totally organized activities for children. If you were out as a child, you were often just playing with someone on the block within earshot of your house. Sports meant sandlot ball. Practices and games melted together and there were few organized teams.

It may be hard for your parents not to interfere if they think you are being overly permissive with your children. Depending on how traditional your parents are, the outcome can run anywhere from "Boy, times are certainly different" to "Why don't you control those kids?" It is a different world for you than it was for them and sometimes it's hard for the two to meet.

Discuss possible problems—yours, your parents, and your kids—before your parents move in. Warn your parents if you do not schedule the kids the way they did you. Let them know that curfews and amounts of freedom allowed are things you, your partner, and your children have discussed and agreed on. If any new activity in the house is going to be a problem to the family as a whole, discuss the alternatives beforehand. Everyone, however, parents, partner, and children, should be responsible for making any changes as minor and as easy as possible.

The Kids

Most single-family homes occupied by a family cannot accommodate extra people without at least some shifting around. This shifting, in most cases, will be done by the children. They need to be involved in the decision-making process. Their needs, wants, and fears should be addressed and, if at all possible, worked out to their satisfaction.

Young Children

Young children who know and love their grandparents will probably see no reason for discussion. Young children want the people they love close to them and the idea of having Grandma or Grandpa in the same house with them will probably seem very exciting.

My children were very young when Grandma moved in. They really couldn't discuss the move. They were too young. They were just delighted to have Grandma living with us. (S.L.)

Young children do, however, need to be reminded that the arrival of Grandma or Grandpa (or both) will be accompanied by some changes in household routine. Does Grandma regularly take a nap during which time the children will need to be a little more quiet? Tell the children this. Ask for their suggestions about how to handle this time. Does Grandpa get irritated with loud noises? Will the children need to play the TV or their radios a bit more quietly? Is Grandma or Grandpa hard of hearing? Will it bother the kids to have the radio or TV blasting something they didn't choose? Do Grandma and Grandpa have certain bathroom routines that it will be hard for them to change? Will meal times need to be changed to accommodate the grandparents' dietary needs?

These are all disruptions in a child's life. They are not major, and they can be worked out to everyone's satisfaction, but do talk to the children about them. Your children need to know that this is their home and that you value their feelings and their suggestions. They need to feel they have helped solve a problem in their family.

Older Children

Pre-teens and teens are much more likely to have strong opinions on the subject of the grandparents moving in than are the little children. The teen years are touchy years for most kids. Their emotions are more volatile and confusion usually reigns supreme in all areas of their lives. The addition of grandparents to the household is yet another major change at a time of their lives fraught with daily major changes. This does not mean, however, that teenagers are going to necessarily object to the idea of their grandparents moving in. It simply means they will probably be more aware that there will need to be changes made in their lives as well as in the lives of the rest of the family to accommodate the change. Include your teenagers in every phase of the decision-making process. Ask them what their fears are.

> We talked about Grandma coming to live with us and the kids were very willing to have Grandma in our home. This did not mean, however, that they were willing to cut down on their activities. They really didn't expect Grandma to do anything for them, they just thought life should go on as usual, and they were right. They figured that Grandma could slide right in as part of the family. (V.T.)

By the time your children are teenagers, your parents may have aged to the point that they are starting to have some health problems. Teenagers are very self-conscious people. Are there any health problems that your parents have that your teenagers may find embarrassing? Is Grandma starting to experience memory loss? Is Grandpa hard of hearing? Do either of them have bladder-control problems? Do they have false teeth? If so, do they wear them?

Find out before the move. Tell the kids what physical problems will be involved. Get their reactions and feelings. You don't want to find out six months later that your daughter never brings friends home because she doesn't want her friends to see Grandma without her teeth.

> My father-in-law had prostate surgery. He had to wear a catheter for a while. It was strange. He really didn't seem too embarrassed by it, but the kids did. It wasn't that it

embarrassed them. It was more that they just assumed it embarrassed him so they were embarrassed for him. They didn't bring their friends around until it was gone. (P.M.)

If the situation with elderly parents is approached realistically and with open minds, your teenagers can learn much from their new extended family. Two of the most valuable things your teenagers can learn in living with their grandparents are patience and empathy. Young people are always in a hurry. Walking and talking slowly can be a torture for them, but they probably will have to learn to move more slowly when dealing with their grandparents. This can be frustrating for them, but it is also good for them. Remind your teenagers that their grandparents were young once themselves. Show them family pictures of Grandma and Grandpa as young adults. It is probably hard for you to think of your parents as young. If it is hard for you, it is impossible, without help, for your children.

Try to get your teenagers to picture their grandparents as young and full of energy. Remind the kids that if it is frustrating for them to slow down for Grandma or Grandpa, then it must be thousands of times more frustrating for the grandparents. After all, the kids can resume normal speed once they have finished with the grandparents. The grandparents will never be able to go back to the health and energy levels they were used to when they were young.

My sixteen-year-old daughter took Grandma to the store for soda. My daughter is one of those kids who is in perpetual motion. She does everything at top speed. She couldn't see why Grandma had to go to the store to begin with. She was willing to go for the soda. Grandma wanted to go because it was something to do. Anyway, by the time they got back, they weren't speaking to each other. My daughter was too fast for Grandma and Grandma was too slow for my daughter. I had to sit my daughter down and remind her that Grandma simply couldn't move any faster.

In this case, my daughter would have to be the one to make the necessary adjustment. It's sometimes very hard for me, let alone the kids, to remember this. (K.V.)

What Do You Think, Kids?

The more you can find out from your children before the move, the less trouble you will have after. Ask your children pointed questions. Assure them that you need them to be honest in their answers and that you will do your best to be objective.

How do you think Grandma/Grandpa should spend their time?

Does Grandma/Grandpa do anything that confuses you?

Does anything about Grandma/Grandpa or their physical condition scare you?

What would you like to know about the thing that scares you that would make you less afraid?

What are you most looking forward to by having Grandma/Grandpa live here?

What do you think Grandma/Grandpa should do for themselves?

What extra tasks are you willing to do for me if I need more time to help them?

How do you feel about the changes (changing bedrooms, sharing bedrooms, etc.) you will have to make in the house?

If you don't like the changes, what do you suggest we do instead?

Are there any possible future situations (sickness, death, etc.) that worry you?

What would you want to know that could help with these fears or worries?

How would you suggest we handle problems that arise?

How much say do you think you should have in this whole situation?

Do you think we are handling this situation fairly so far?

If you don't think we are being fair, what do you suggest we do instead?

Do you feel that I will be fair with you if you have a problem with Grandma/Grandpa?

Is there anything of importance that you feel we have not taken care of?

Review

Don't assume that either your parents or your partner will relish the idea of moving in together.

Find out what your parents' major fears concerning such a move are.

Find out what your partner's major fears concerning such a move are.

Realistically look at the relationship your parents and partner have built. Don't try to force either party into a living arrangement they can't possibly enjoy.

Include your brothers and sisters in discussions about moving your parents in. Find out anything they have noticed about your parents that may be of help to you.

Insist that your brothers and sister share the responsibility of caring for your parents.

Include the children in your discussion about moving your parents in.

Find out your children's main concerns.

Point out any health problems your parents may have that your children need to deal with.

Make sure the children understand that you will be open-minded about any problems they may have concerning the grandparents.

10

COMBINING TWO HOUSEHOLDS

The year after we bought our house, we decided to renovate and enlarge the kitchen. Being fairly masochistic like
many homeowners, we did the work ourselves. About a
month after we started the work, we had gotten to the bare-
bones stage. I was, by this time, on intimate terms with the
interior spaces of the walls and there was a gaping six-foot-
long trench in the floor that went clear through to the basement. I swore that if I actually lived through the renovation, I
would never, ever change anything in the house again. I lived
to renovate again.

Any changes to your home will need to be discussed,
agreed upon, and made before you bring your parent or
parents in. Most of the considerations may seem obvious, but
it will help, in any case, to go over them here.

"In-law" Apartments

The in-law apartment is an idea that has been around for
years. The basic idea is to create a space in your home with a
living room, kitchenette, and a bedroom that your parents
can move into and call their own. Many homes on the market

advertise "in-laws" as a selling point. Although the in-law space is ideal, the physical arrangements are usually impossible to use. The majority of houses that boast "in-laws" are older homes with an apartment fixed up in what used to be the attic. In some cases the "in-law" is in the basement. Both of these areas can only be reached by a staircase. In older homes, the attic and basement staircases are almost always fairly narrow and very steep. The original builders had storage and furnaces in mind when these spaces were designed. If storage is the only use for an attic or a basement, narrow stairs are probably fine. After all, you only have to use them twice a year during the holidays to get and then to replace the decorations. You might use them during the spring when the cleaning bug hits. These staircases were definitely not designed for elderly people in good or bad health.

Our own house is an example. We own a 60-year-old bungalow. These houses were a very popular style years ago. They had enormous attics. Most of those attics have since been converted to bedroom space for growing families. This was one of the strong points of this type of construction. Our house was listed as having an "in-law" and it certainly did. The upstairs had one, small, oddly shaped bedroom; one medium-sized, oddly shaped living room; a bathroom; and a tiny kitchen with a tiny sink and a tiny gas stove. The kids thought it was great. The kids were also the only ones who could go up the stairs comfortably since the steps were narrow, very dark, and almost straight up. The stairs struck me more as a carpeted ladder than as a staircase. I had trouble with the stairs. There is no way either my husband's mother or my parents could have gone up and down those stairs and lived to tell about it. About the only way we could have used our "in-law" was to put our parents upstairs and leave them there, never again to be seen on the first floor.

The stairs were too narrow to install a lift. In addition to the construction problems with the stairs, lifts cost several thousand dollars which we did not have. The only reasonable solution was for the kids to move upstairs, leaving the downstairs bedrooms for those not athletic enough to make the stairs. The kids loved it. The kids also loved the little stove and the little sink, both of which we removed so we could sleep at night. I don't know about you, but the thought of budding chefs practicing on a gas stove in the middle of the night was more than my nervous system could handle. So much for our "in-law" apartment.

"In-law" apartments in the basement share many of the same problems as the upstairs variety. The only saving grace to basement apartments is they may actually be on ground level. If not on ground level, outside basement stairs are usually wider and not as long and steep as their inside counterparts. The problem with outdoor stairs is that they are exposed to the weather and your parents may not want to go outside every time they feel the urge to come up and visit.

Everyone I interviewed had found space on the main level of their homes for their parents with one exception. That person had arranged for a bedroom on the first floor but her father chose to take an empty bedroom on the second floor. This second floor was not, however, a converted attic. It was the floor on which all of the bedrooms were located. The staircase is wide, well lighted, and has a reasonable degree of incline.

Where Will Your Parents Sleep?

The Spare Room. If only one parent is moving in, the obvious answer to this question is "in the spare room." It's obvious, of course, only if you happen to have a spare room. If not, what then?

The usual answer to this is to move one or more of the kids into a space that was either the bedroom of one or to move one or more of the kids into a space that was not previously a bedroom. If your children are conveniently of the same sex, doubling up in one room may be the easiest answer. You may have to do some conniving with the kids to get their full cooperation, but it can usually be done without too much bribing. If, on the other hand, the kids were thoughtless enough to be a boy and a girl, other arrangements will have to be made. It is not fair or particularly healthy to put a sister and a brother permanently in the same room. They have different needs for privacy and it is essential for their mental and emotional health to honor those needs. There are, of course, many variations:

> When my mother moved in, we merely moved one of the kids to another room and redecorated the room for my mother. The kids didn't mind. Actually, they must have some Gypsy blood because they switched rooms every six months or so anyway. This move didn't faze them at all. (P.M.)

> There were no space problems when my father moved in. There is plenty of space for everyone. My father took one of the empty bedrooms. (K.H.)

> We had no spare room. I had to put my mother in the same room with one of my daughters. We had six kids at home at the time and one who was in a home for the developmentally disabled. He would come home on weekends. Ma had a hard time coping with all the kids. We couldn't add on, we had no money. We just had to make do. (V.M.)

Do you have a TV room that can be converted into a bedroom? How about a basement? Basements can be fun. Since they're off the beaten track, boys especially can create rugged bedrooms out of basement spaces that not only fill the need but spur their imaginations. If you are moving the boys to the basement, let them use their imaginations to decorate their new room. As long as the basement is dry and warm, many inexpensive but creative things can be done to create new bedroom space.

Separate Bedrooms

If both your parents are moving in, you may be faced with a different problem. Some elderly people choose to sleep in separate bedrooms. There can be any number of reasons for this, but the most common one is that their sleeping schedules changed over the years. When there was no longer a need to get up for work, perhaps one found that he or she enjoyed staying up to watch the late-late movie and the other was an early sleeper and early riser. Perhaps one is a late-night reader, and the light bothered the other one. In a home where the children are grown and gone, there is usually at least one bedroom to spare. The sleeping problems were solved by one or the other moving into an empty room.

If this is the case, it may be very hard for your parents to learn to sleep in the same room again. You may find it necessary to add onto your home to make more room. The question that becomes very important at this point is "Who's going to pay for major changes?"

This is something that will definitely need to be settled before anything else is done. Although many partners will agree to move your parents into their homes, putting out large sums of money to do so is a different matter entirely.

Additions

If you can find no spare room for your parents, an addition may be the only answer. Additions to an existing house often add to the value of the house so this answer will usually, in the long run, pay for itself. You will probably need financial help in the short run, though.

Tell your parents of the space problems that exist and ask for their suggestions. If they are planning to sell the house they are living in, they may be able to finance the changes to your home. However, since you will be the one who gains the equity in your home through major improvement, you may want to offer to split the cost with them.

If your parents haven't any money and you have brothers and sisters, ask them to chip in. This is, after all, a family problem that should be handled as such. In a family with several grown children, no one child should be expected to do everything.

ECHO Homes

One solution being proposed around this country which is already in use in Australia is ECHO homes. These are pre-fab homes supplied at a set price by a housing authority and set on the property of a family member of the aged person. This provides the aging family member a home of his or her own in close proximity to the family of an adult child. Although these homes can answer many problems, zoning regulations in many places prohibit their use. The basic principal, however, is very good and work is being done on exempting ECHO housing from existing zoning laws.

In all places that now use such housing, certain rules are fairly standard. First, the ECHO home must be placed on the property of a blood relative. Second, the house is merely leased, not owned. Once there is no more need for the house, it is removed from the property. With these regulations in place, there should be no problem with future property values since the homes are temporary. In most places where they are in use, the homes can be constructed to match the style of the existing house.

The real advantages of these homes are that they come equipped with appliances and fixtures and can be assembled in less than a week, sometimes in only one day. In this country, information about ECHO housing can be obtained by writing the American Association of Retired Persons (AARP). The address of this organization is 1909 K Street, Washington, D.C. 20049. (Many communities have local AARP offices.)

Selling

If no one has the money to add on to your existing house, you may want to consider selling both your home and the home of your parents to finance a larger home that will accommodate everyone comfortably. This, however, should be a last resort, due to the obvious problems involved. No one I interviewed found it necessary to do this.

Everyone interviewed managed to find and use existing space in their own homes. One family did add a dormer to their second floor to expand it. This was done with an eye to the future of their growing family, however, before the mother moved in. In our case, everyone shifted and we remodeled the upstairs to accommodate my office, but no extra space was added.

> We raised the roof on our house to add more bedrooms, but that was because our family was growing. It just happened to work out well for my mother. Now my husband and I and our daughters have rooms upstairs and my mother has two rooms on the first floor. She uses one as a bedroom and one as a TV room. It works out well. We offered, when we were raising the roof, to raise the whole roof and put a bedroom, sitting room, and bath on the second floor for her, but she didn't want that. She didn't want to deal with stairs. (S.L.)

Medical Equipment

Another consideration when moving parents into your home is their present and future health. Will they need medical equipment, and if so, how much will there be and how big is it?

At the start of our experience with my mother, she had only one small machine to give herself breathing treatments. Before she passed away, there was a hospital bed, a wheelchair, oxygen tanks, another oxygen machine, and a suction machine. One more piece of equipment, and we would have found it necessary to break out a wall to make more room.

Keep your parents' future health in mind when you are moving them in. Try not to put them in a bedroom with a strange turn in it or at the end of a narrow hallway. Wheelchairs take a lot of space to move and maneuver.

Emergency Equipment

Most people feel more secure when fast medical emergency help is available. The efforts, however, of the best paramedics can be hampered by barriers in the home. Stretchers are big and clumsy. Room is needed to maneuver them in and out. It becomes even more traumatic for an elderly sick person when they have to be hand carried down a flight of stairs, or even down a narrow corridor to a stretcher that couldn't make the turn. I know from experience with my mother that it is awfully stressful for the family to watch as a stretcher is stood on end with an elderly person strapped to it because the doorway is too narrow to get it out any other way.

Choosing Medical Equipment
If medical equipment does become a necessity, shop around. There are many versions of the different kinds of equipment available. Usually the newer equipment is more compact and easier to manage.

In our case, my mother reached a point that she needed oxygen constantly. Our first experience was with tanks. Two huge tanks that look something like torpedoes and stood five feet tall were delivered to the house. These tanks were too heavy for me to move and needed large metal collars around the bases to keep them stable. They took up quite a bit of room and required a complete reorganization of Mom's room. Finally a kindly respiratory therapist recommended an oxygen concentrator. This is a machine about the size of a portable dehumidifier that generates its own oxygen by concentrating a certain amount of the air in the room. It was much smaller and easier to move. We did, of course, keep an emergency tank in case of power failure or machine break-down, but this tank didn't have to be in the bedroom. Concentrators had been available all along, but we did not know they existed. Had we known from the beginning, less furniture shifting would have been necessary.

A good source of information about hospital supplies is the social service agency of the hospital from which your doctor practices. These are dedicated, knowledgeable people who can make you aware of the many home-health services available to you and your parent.

Bathrooms and Back Doors

Two problems which are often mutually exclusive seem to arise again and again. One is the need for the elderly, especially the sickly elderly, to be near a bathroom. Many elderly people have trouble sleeping through the night. If they can't sleep, they are more than likely to make many trips to the bathroom. The closer they can be to the bathroom the more secure they feel, and closeness to the bathroom affords added privacy for both the elderly person and the family. Multiple trips are easier and less embarrassing if they do not take the person through the living room or the kitchen. The problem with closeness to the bathroom is that bathrooms are usually placed in hallways between bedrooms. These hallways are almost never big enough for stretchers and wheelchairs to move freely. The ideal setup would be a back bedroom near the rear door of the house with a bathroom of its own. Unfortunately this is not something most houses come equipped with.

Review

Find out how many rooms will be needed.

Check out your house for existing space that can be used.

Decide beforehand who will need to move around.

If the changes will cost money, all family members of the parents involved should chip in to help pay for the changes. It is a family problem—not just your problem.

Keep the future health of the parents in mind when choosing spaces. Medical equipment is bulky.

Try to locate your parent near a bathroom.

11

GETTING READY TO MOVE

My first memory of moving from one house to another is
one of rush and chaos. My parents had sold our home more
quickly than they had expected and before they found a new
home. It became a race to find and buy a home before we had
to leave the old one. Since my mother never left us with
sitters, we went on all trips to look for a new house. On one of
these excursions, my uncle was driving. My mother, brother,
and I were in the back seat. My uncle lit a cigar. Unfortunately
the combination of the cigar and the back seat were too much
for my six-year-old stomach. I was sure I'd be killed if a threw
up all over my uncle's car, so I quietly opened the sleeve of my
mother's coat, which she was wearing at the time, and threw
up down the sleeve. To this day, the idea of moving affects me
the same way. I start to look for a sleeve to throw up into. I'm
sure I'm not alone in this.

The stage of choosing what to move can be the most difficult, but it can also be the most therapeutic. It is, however, a
stage that will take much patience and understanding. It
will, in many cases, be a time of laughter and a time of tears

as the possessions of a lifetime are reviewed, discussed, dissected, and in many cases, discarded.

Father's Things

Your father's things will probably not cause much of a problem. Most of the people I talked to about their fathers and what they wanted to bring with them said that there was very little that they wanted. Most men don't seem to become as emotionally attached to things as women do. In one case, it was only a bedroom set and a couple of couches that came with the father. In my own father's case, the only thing I remember him arguing about were old shoes. He could see no reason to throw his old shoes away even though he hadn't worn them in 15 years and they were permanently shaped to the shoe rack. The shoes went and he never really missed them.

> He had his own furniture. He brought his bedroom set and furnished his room and also furnished some of my rooms with additional furniture. For example, the sitting room that leads to our bedroom was completely unfurnished and he brought the furniture from his apartment and furnished the sitting room. That was never a point of contention. There were many things that were discarded and I had lots of input into that. Many things were given away. He brought the best and furnished his room and some of my rooms. It worked out beautifully. He asked my opinion on all of it. (K.H.)

Mother's Things

As mentioned, it seems more difficult for females to give up their things than men. In most households, it was the female who decorated. The husband may have been very involved with selecting and purchasing the furniture, but the furniture is not the most problematic area. It is all of the little things that go into making a house a home that become areas of debate.

In our case, my parents had lived in the same home for 35 years. I was counting on the fact that it was a fairly small house to have solved some of the problems I could foresee. I really didn't remember how much my mother had packed into that small home. Mom was a keeper. Little knickknacks meant a great deal to her. She cherished everything anyone had given her.

The only difference between a big house and a small house is that in a big house you can put these cherished mementos on display. They are out for everyone to see. You know what you will be dealing with. In a small house, this may not be possible. When the time came to start organizing and packing for the move, I was flabbergasted at the amount of things my mother had packed away in boxes for safekeeping. She had every photo, every report card, every little picture and painting from the grandchildren that she had ever received.

There seems to be no way to get through the organizing and discarding of a lifetime of collected objects without stirring up emotions. There are a few things that can be done, however, to minimize the emotional pitfalls that this stage is fraught with. We discovered these different approaches through much trial and error. The error parts never failed to cause flare-ups and second thoughts about the whole idea.

My Treasures, Your Trash

One of the biggest problems you'll face at the sorting and packing stage is that you and your parent are two different people. You have different tastes, different memories, and different things you cherish. One example of this in our case was the Dutch oven.

I freely admit that my cooking abilities range fair to foul. I have a tendency to forget that I put things on the stove. I also have a severe reluctance to reading cookbooks. I could never in my wildest nightmares conceive of ever becoming attached to a cooking utensil. I truly consider everything produced for use in the kitchen, with the possible exception of the coffee pot, an instrument of torture. So when I found myself in a heated argument over an ancient Dutch oven, I honestly couldn't understand it. My mother wanted the Dutch oven. I have my own which was much newer than her 50-year-old-with-a-broken-handle model. She fought for her Dutch oven. I fought to throw it out. Before we were through, we were both practically in tears. That was some Dutch oven. I'm a bit slow sometimes, but it wasn't really a Dutch oven we were fighting over—it was a lifetime.

That Dutch oven represented many things to my mother. First, it was in its day one of the best on the market. My mother was a very frugal person. That oven represented a flight from the usual. She bought the best instead of the least costly. Then it was chili parties on Saturday nights. My parents couldn't afford to go out much as was true of most of their family members and friends. My mom made a wicked chili. As young marrieds, my mom and dad had gotten into the habit of having their friends over for chili. It was cheap, it was filling, it was good, and it came to represent friendship and close family bonds. The Dutch oven and chili were one and the same. Over the years, the Dutch oven helped to stretch soups and stews. She knew that pot and knew exactly how much heat it could bear. It had become a friend that she could rely on.

To me, the Dutch oven was an old broken pot—garbage. I had insulted her friend. Worse yet, I had insulted her memories.

The Dutch oven served her one more time before she moved out of her home. That Dutch oven helped me to begin to see her things through her eyes. I became less practical about what we kept and what we threw away and started to evaluate the worth of things by their history and emotional impact rather than if it was something we could use or not.

She had some bowls—crockery. One especially. It's in my kitchen because she wants that bowl in my kitchen. I'm afraid to use the darn thing. If I ever broke it she'd kill me.

It was her mother's bowl. It's a crockery mixing bowl and they chip so easily. My daughter came out with it once and I had to tell her not to use it. She asked, "What's it there for if we can't use it?" I said, "It's there so we will know that it's there. Just don't use it!"

My Home Is Your Home

Learning to look at things through your parent's eyes is one of the most important steps in this home-combining process. Ask your parent what each thing means to him or her and why. It is at this point that we stop moving Mom or Dad into our house and start the process of combining homes to make a new and, it is to be hoped, for everyone involved, a better home.

This, as I said, was my own biggest hurdle. Being the biggest, once it was conquered, everything ran more smoothly. On my part, this meant that I had to suppress the feeling that I was doing my parents a big favor and encourage the feeling that I was simply asking them to join our household as family members. Once I could establish this thought firmly, the thought that my mother should discard many of her mementos eased to the point that we could find workable compromises.

Large pieces of furniture are almost always the first things to be talked about. Who has the better furniture? You or your parents? Often your parents' furniture will be older and possibly in poorer condition than yours. Elderly people on fixed incomes rarely buy new furniture or go to the expense of having the old furniture reupholstered. Be honest but tactful. Do not assume that your mother will be delighted that you see her furniture as perfect for furnishing the basement. She and your father probably worked for a long time to get that furniture and they may just see it as an insult for it to end up in a basement. If you cannot use the larger pieces of furniture, it may be a good idea to suggest that you ask around the family to see if there is anyone who would need and appreciate it. Most people don't really mind giving furniture away if they know someone can use it.

> She [my mother] didn't want her front-room furniture, however, she did bring her tables. They were in my basement until just recently. I am using two of them temporarily. My sister took the dining-room set and a friend took the kitchen table. I took the single bed that used to be mine. (S.L.)

> When my mother moved in, she had very few things to bring with her. She did have an old couch and chair and we put those in the basement. (P.M.)

It is with the smaller things—pictures, knickknacks, kitchen utensils— that you, at the receiving end, will need to be more flexible.

Everyone's Got to Give

If the problem of possessions is faced as a family, all will turn out for the best. This may be the time to remind your parents of things they are saving for the grandchildren. Why not give them these things now? In this way, the grandparents will be able to see their delight instead of knowing that the gift will bring sorrow because it means a loved one is gone. My mother had the grandchildren go through her junk jewelry and take what they wanted. In most cases they really didn't want anything, but they had a good laugh with Grandma going through the stuff. It had served its purpose— giving them all a little joy—and she didn't mind throwing away what they didn't want.

Organizing the Inventory

Start your organizing by marking off zones. For example, start with a "throw-away zone." Put anything that is not needed, is in poor repair, and gets no emotional response in the throw-away zone. Throw away everything in this zone every day before anyone has a chance for second thoughts.

Zone 2 may be the "give-to-family" zone. In this zone you would place anything that is in good repair that might be of use to someone else in the family. Make a list of these items and contact family members about them. Give people a reasonable time to collect anything they may be interested in. Don't, however, leave this time span open. Set a limit of one or two weeks at the most.

My niece got the little microwave and my sister needed an iron. We went through everything like that. Whoever in the family needed or wanted the things my mother could no longer use took them. (S.L.)

If the items are not taken, shift them to the throw-away zone or to zone 3—"the garage-sale zone." The garage-sale zone will be the place for anything that is in good repair, of no emotional significance, and reasonably salable.

If you are not up to a garage sale, zone 3 can easily become the "charity zone." Choose your favorite charity that accepts household items, the Salvation Army or AMVETS, for example. Arrange pickup for a time when you will be finished with the sorting.

The final zone—zone 4—is the tricky one. In this space put all of those things that seem to have an emotional impact on your parent. Once you have cleared the house of the items in the other three zones, start going over everything put in this zone. If possible, take your time. Enjoy reminiscing with your parent over the items in this group. Be prepared to agree to keep everything in this group. It isn't fair to ask a person, any person, but especially a person you love, to give up the mementos of a lifetime. If one of your parents has passed away, these mementos may be all the other one has to remember them by. Keep reminding yourself that your memories and your parent's are not the same.

She brought all her pictures. My father's pictures and her pictures of her mother. She also brought what was left of her mother's good china. There are many things she brought that we still have in boxes. (S.L.)

This may seem obvious and you may think that you would have no problem with this. However, as this pile grows, and you start to panic at the idea of trying to find places for everything in your home, you may find yourself pushing to have these things transferred into the "throw-away zone." I did, with, as I said before, sad results.

The problem that arose was not in regards to what she had brought with her. The problem that came up was with the items she had left for safekeeping at my sister's home. She would express a desperate need for a particular item, always at an inconvenient time for me or my wife. She would harp until either my wife or I would drive her to my sister's house to pick up one item. After several such trips, we moved everything to our home. (P.M.)

One way I found that helped me to overcome the push to toss things was to find something in my house that I was emotionally very attached to. In my case, it was a broken ceramic penny bank. A cheap little thing, but cute. I had given it to an aunt as a joke. She got a big kick out of it. We laughed on many occasions about that bank. When she passed away, I took the bank back. It is on a table in my living room. It matches nothing in the house. When I would become particularly frustrated with the growing mounds of things in the "keep" pile at my mother's house, I would go home and look at the bank. Then I would ask myself the same questions every time: Is that bank valuable? No! Is that bank pretty? No! Does that bank enhance the "decor" of this room? No! What would you say if someone told you to throw it away? "I'll break your legs first!" is what I would say. That private little question-and- answer session never failed to help me understand my mother's feelings about her things.

No matter how frustrating the sorting and packing is, it does finally come to an end. The next step is to incorporate as much as you can into your parents' new home.

Some of Mine + Some of Yours = Ours

In order for your parents to feel like family members rather than boarders, they will need some space. This space cannot be limited to a bedroom. In your home, you do not keep everything that is important to you in one room. You spread it out so that no matter where you are in the house, you know you are home. Luckily, the things that make us feel most at home are usually not very big.

Look around your home. Are there pictures on the wall that you like but are not emotionally attached to? Are these possible areas in which your parents' pictures could be hung? Can you find space among your knickknacks to put your mother's favorite figurines, vases, and plates? If you are anything like I am, there are plenty of knickknacks around your house that you don't even particularly like but haven't gotten around to tossing or putting in a garage sale. These are the things that can be moved to make room for your parents' things.

While you are doing this, try to keep in mind that it really doesn't matter if you don't particularly like your parent's taste in art or knickknacks. You are doing it not for the objects but for the people. You might also want to keep in mind that you probably gave them some of the very things you are now looking at in dismay. Bear with it. The feeling of family that comes through compromising favorite things is well worth having to look at a statuette that does not fit your taste in art.

Some of the things she brought, like her mother's dishes, some plates and cups now have an honored place in my china cabinet. Her pictures and some other things we hung on the walls. We still haven't found a place for some of her mementos, like gifts from her fortieth and fiftieth anniversary parties, but we'll find places for them. (S.L.)

One of the nicest days we had after my parents moved in had to do with Mom's pictures and knickknacks. While she was sleeping, my husband replaced several pictures we had in the dining room with pictures my mother had painted. We also put up the sketch my cousin had done of my parents for their fiftieth wedding anniversary. We also, as a surprise, decided to keep a hutch that we at first felt we didn't have room for. She thought it was gone. We set the hutch up and filled it as it had been in her home, with presents she had received over the years. She was delighted when she got up and found "her things were truly about her." She felt at home and that is exactly where she was.

Review

Be prepared for emotional upset.

Give yourself enough time for a leisurely packing job.

Put things in three or four groups—a throw-away group, a give-away-to-family group, a garage-sale group, and a keep group.

Be prepared to keep anything of emotional significance to your parent.

Urge your parents to give anything they had set aside for the grandchildren to them now.

Be patient.

Find places around your home for your parents' mementos and knickknacks.

12

CHANGING LIFESTYLES

My dad was a meat-and-potatoes man. Every night we would have some kind of red meat (he didn't like fish or chicken), potatoes, and vegetables. Dinner was on the table promptly at 6:00 when he walked in from work. The world could be falling apart, but dinner was on the table at 6:00 and all family members had to be there, unless they had a very, very good excuse.

One of the most obvious differences in your family life and that of your parents will probably be in how your family approaches mealtimes. These differences can cause problems unless they are acknowledged and dealt with.

Your Grandparents

If your parents are now in their seventies or eighties, their parents were the first generation to see modern conveniences come into the home. A person who is 80 now was probably born at home and may have been raised, at least for a while, in a home without electricity, running water, and indoor plumbing. Your grandmothers probably spent most of their day cooking and cleaning with precious little time between the cleanup of one meal and the cooking of the next. Large families were common in the early 1900s and life was centered around family. Although some families had radios, no one had televisions. The fathers went to work and usually came home at the same time every day. The wife and mother was expected to run the home and prepare meals. Families generally ate together at specified times. All this was assumed, and departure from it usually raised eyebrows and started tongues wagging in the neighborhood. Neighborhoods themselves were different then. People knew each other. With no air-conditioning in the summer, people sat outside to keep cool. Neighbors knew what went on in each other's homes. Often, in case of illness in the family, the neighbors helped the family out by bringing food and giving their time until the crisis was past. This is not as common today.

Your Parents

Your 70- and 80-year-old parents were the young adults of the Depression. They knew hardship and appreciated the safety and sanity that family brought in those frightening times. The Depression was followed by World War II. Families were broken apart as the men were sent to war. Old traditions began to die. Women started to work outside the home on a wholesale basis for the first time in history.

After the war, suburbs started to become the desired place to live and raise a family. A newfound prosperity made this possible. By the time you came along, probably in the mid- to late Forties, family life was in full swing again but very different from the lives your parents had led. More people could afford cars. Postwar industries were growing and provided a life-style unknown before the war. Although many women chose to remain in the work force, the norm of the day was that the wife stayed home and raised the children while the husband commuted to the city to work. Again, family dinners were the thing. Husbands came home from work, wives had dinner on the table, and the children were expected to be there. Although schools did offer extra-curricular activities, they were usually limited to sports. Television shows of the time depicted close-knit suburban families with mother, father, and children discussing the day's events at dinner each evening. The wives were always depicted as housewives rather than working mothers and they and their homes were always immaculate. All problems faced by these families could be solved in thirty minutes or less. This was the ideal family of the Fifties. Chances are your family did not quite live up to the ideal set in these shows, but many of the family patterns shown were probably being enforced in your home. Dinner at six, cooked by your full-time housewife/mother was not at all unusual.

> Dinners in our house when I was growing up were grue-some. My dad was the breadwinner. My mom stayed home. Dad didn't want her to work and she did what Dad wanted. Dinner was the same time every evening and the food was entirely geared to Dad's preferences. It was also the time my Dad would question us kids about what we did during the day. I can't remember one dinner in my father's house that was pleasant. One of us always did something during the day that would upset him at dinner. It was terri-ble, but it was on time. If nothing else, dinner was always on time. (K. V.)

You and Me

Now we come to you and me. You probably do not have a home in which it is possible to put dinner on the table at the same time every evening, cooked from scratch by your own loving hands. There are some very good reasons for this. Today's housing prices make it very hard for a family to own its own home on one salary. In most cases, this means the mother is working outside the home. If the mother is work-ing, she probably doesn't have the hours needed to prepare dinner from scratch every evening. Another difference today is the number of after-school activities available to children. Where once parks only offered space to run and play, most park districts today offer a whole list of activities for children. Your children may be involved in some of these programs. If they are, they are probably away from home during dinner at least one day a week.

> We don't have regular time schedules. We're all involved in a lot of activities. We probably have two regularly scheduled meals a week as a family. Definitely on Sunday and perhaps one other evening. Other than that, there are evenings that I go back to work so I eat quickly. The kids are starving when they come home from school so they sometimes eat then. If the older one has a music lesson or softball practice, dinner is after that. My husband gets home anywhere from 6:00 to 9:00 so he eats then. We all eat at different times. (K.H.)

The families of your grandparents were busy around their own homes. The families of today are busy with outside activities. Washers and dryers have erased the need for a whole day devoted to the wash. Your grandmother probably had to bake her own bread. You pick up bread and milk on your way home from work. Cooking, for most rushed people, needs to be accomplished quickly and efficiently so the family can get on with their activities. Conveniently frozen foods, microwaves, and gas ovens make it possible to make dinner quickly. Where Grandma perhaps needed two or three hours to prepare and cook a meal, you can accomplish dinner in much less than an hour.

What You're Used To

Our parents often think we run our homes the same way they ran theirs. Quite a few people I talked to mentioned that dinner time was a major source of irritation both for them and for the parents who had moved in. Either dinner was too disorganized for their parents to cope with, or the food we find on today's tables did not suit their tastes.

If your parents insisted that the whole family be present and accounted for at dinner time, and you don't feel this is necessary, it may be a source of problems. My family is a perfect example of the types of problems that can arise.

For all our married lives, my husband worked for the Chicago Police Department. He, like the majority of police officers, changed shifts every month. One month he would work days, the next four to midnight, the next, midnight to seven in the morning. Our meal schedules, or lack thereof, also shifted monthly. I also worked full-time, first as a teacher and then as an editor. The children were used to the shifts in schedule. Sometimes we ate at a normal hour (by normal I mean anywhere between five and eight p.m.). As the kids got older and more involved in sports and part-time jobs, a new, unspoken rule went into effect. If there were less than three (counting myself) home at dinner time, I didn't cook. We went out for fast food or fended for ourselves with whatever was available in the fridge.

In the years directly preceding my husband's retirement, all the kids were old enough to take care of themselves and we rarely had family dinners. I often used the 4:00-to-midnight month as a time to visit friends and would go out to dinner with them often. This was also my take-a-nap-after-work month. Scheduled dinners became almost nonexistent. Then my parents came to live with us.

My dad had always worked a nine-to-five job. My mother always had dinner on the table at six in the evening, even when she worked. We were expected to be there. If my brother had football practice, my mother kept his dinner warm. True, as we got older and held part-time jobs, we weren't always home for dinner, but dinner was still on the table at six.

When my parents moved in, it never dawned on me that expectations about dinner would cause major problems. One of the reasons they moved in was that my mother no longer had the strength to cope with the house and cooking. My father had never been in a position where he had to do housework and cook. At 82 it seemed unreasonable to expect him to learn these new skills. I knew their coming would require regular meals, but I hadn't really thought about the strain it would cause to have those meals at the same time every day.

I make my living as a free-lance writer and editor and I work from my home. The situation seemed ideal. Unfortunately, my idea of a schedule being dinner at six, give or take an hour or two, didn't go over well. My parents were used to eating at the same time every day and they found it extremely difficult to veer from that schedule. In their defense, neither one of them was terribly healthy. My dad is diabetic so mealtimes took on an importance I wasn't used to. He developed the diabetes after I was married and gone, so I wasn't thinking of mealtimes as part of a preventative health-care program. You ate when you were hungry.

Not so any more. My mother was on many medications. Regular mealtimes were also a necessity for her. In addition to needing to eat at regular times, they both had specific dietary problems that needed to be addressed.

Dietary Needs

If you are lucky and healthy, being on a diet means you want to lose some weight. To the great majority of elderly people, being on a diet means they have health problems that dictate what they can and cannot eat. My dad's diabetes meant always having fruit in the house and milk for breakfast. My mom couldn't stomach breakfast early in the morning but she couldn't take her medication on an empty stomach. The doctor recommended powdered breakfast drink as a solution. Again, I had to be careful never to run out of milk. These don't seem like big things. But, if your kids are no longer infants, and you run out of milk in the morning, you probably improvise. Even growing children can go without milk for a couple of hours until you can get to the store. When medication is involved this is not always the case.

156

Another area I really hadn't thought about was frozen foods. There were many frozen entrees on the market that my family had come to like. Actually, since my cooking was nothing to write home about, they appreciated the fact that there were companies out there that did a much better job of cooking than I did. We had gotten into the habit (granted, not a good habit) of having frozen main dishes several times a week. I would add a fresh vegetable to these, and since my family is basically healthy, no one seemed to suffer. The one thing all frozen main dishes have too much of, however, is salt. This is also true of most canned foods, especially soup. My mother, as it turns out, was on a salt-restricted diet. Out went the frozen main dishes and most other frozen and canned food. I had to start buying and preparing fresh foods for dinner.

Now, you say, most people already do that. Well, after much searching I had found a husband who actually liked frozen foods. I spent years training my kids to appreciate the wonder of the freezing process. I had gone into debt to buy a microwave. I had even prided myself on the fact that I could make and get dinner on the table in 15 minutes or less. Years of dedicated practice suddenly were tossed out overnight and I had to learn to cook! This, I must say, was a strain on everyone.

My mother likes my cooking, but now has some trouble with it. She's on a low-cholesterol, low-fat diet. She's afraid now to eat some things. She thinks they upset her stomach. I don't think it has to do with her stomach. I think it has to do with her heart. When she was in the hospital one time with an attack of angina, she had extreme amounts of belching. I know it's associated with the heart because she doesn't do it unless her heart is acting up. My cousin would come and bring food—things I didn't know how to fix for her low-fat, low-cholesterol diet. She knew because her brother had open-heart surgery and she did a lot of cooking for him. (S.L.)

I'm a writer. The general public has a picture of people who write, or paint, or do anything in the creative fields as being less than practical and highly forgetful. I am not impractical, but I fostered the idea about forgetfulness. "Oh, did I forget to make dinner?" "Is it that time already?" were not unheard of phrases in my house. Part of it wasn't a put-on. If I was in the middle of writing and things were going well, the last thing I wanted was to stop and break my train of thought, so I usually didn't. By the time I started my writing career, my kids were in high school and college and certainly smart enough not to starve to death because I was upstairs trying to finish something. They expected it and I was more than happy to go along with it, too. My parents, however, were a different matter.

It wasn't that they wouldn't cooperate; it was that they couldn't. I kept forgetting that their inability to prepare meals was one of the reasons we had asked them to come and live with us. This caused considerable tension until we decided to face the problem squarely and try to find a workable compromise. We had a meeting in which my parents told us the things that had to be done at specific times for their health. I explained my feelings about schedules and cooking. We agreed to specific mealtimes. They also agreed to put up with a period of experimentation during which I would try several different convenience-type foods to see how they tolerated them. What finally happened was that we managed to have dinner at the same time every evening, give or take a half hour, and we found a few convenience dishes that suited us all. I did have to make more things than I was used to from scratch, but there were enough products in the convenience line that I no longer felt it was impossible.

Decision-making and Planning

The discussions of time schedules and diets that we had after my parents moved in came after many nasty, frustrating, tearful scenes that could have been avoided. My parents were trying not to be a burden, so they were not telling me about their frustrations. I wasn't paying close enough attention to the differences in their stages in life and their physical health to be aware of the problems. At first, they would have dinner when I put it on the table, and they would eat what I served usually. But there was an underlying tension that kept building until it finally ended with everyone feeling confused and wounded.

What we should have done before they moved in was discuss schedules and specific dietary needs. If you have been living away from your parents' home for a while, you are probably not completely aware of how their day-to-day lives have changed since you moved out. Although my father's diabetes was a given fact, his dietary needs did not seem strange and excessive until the first time I ran out of fruit and didn't bother to go to the store for several days. Trying not to be a burden, he didn't tell me how much he depended on fruit for his sugar balance. Three days later, he was crabby and made the remark that keeping fruit in the house was the least I could do. I thought keeping fruit in the house was the least of my problems. He felt neglected and I felt he was being picky. As soon as he told me why he needed it, I made sure it was always there. Had I known beforehand, it never would have been a problem. To reduce the friction, we ended up with a list of questions like the ones below. Use it as a guide. Discuss these matters before the move, so compromises can be worked out in advance and everyone knows what is expected.

Kitchen Questions

Are you in the habit of eating a hot breakfast?

What time do you eat breakfast?

Can you handle breakfast on your own or do you need someone to make it for you? (My dad has cereal, milk, and fruit for breakfast every morning and takes care of it himself. My mom, however, was losing her eyesight and couldn't find things. She needed help with every meal.)

Do you eat lunch? What? When?

Is there a specific time you want dinner?

Is there any leeway in your dinner schedule?

List the foods you cannot or will not eat.

List the foods you feel are essential in your diet and how you want them cooked.

What about your meal schedules and menus are you willing to change?

What about your meal schedules and menus are you not willing to change?

These are simple common-sense things, but when you are in the middle of something as emotionally trying as moving another person into your home, you can easily overlook them. Unfortunately, it seems to be the simple, everyday things that can cause the most friction.

Tell the Truth and Tell It Now!

A lot of the problems we faced in the beginning were due to the fact that everyone was trying to be unnaturally nice. When we lived in our parents' homes as children and young adults, our parents had no trouble telling us what we were doing wrong and exactly what we could do to remedy the situation. On the other hand, we as children probably didn't hesitate to let our parents know what we wanted and why we were sure we deserved it. Things change when we grow up and they really change when our parents move into our homes. We have a tendency to get so polite that it kills us. I am not suggesting rudeness as an alternative. There is no need or excuse for rudeness either. Simple honesty will do very nicely. Tell your parents that you need to be told what they like and don't like. This is a new situation for them. There will be many things that will come up that they probably never thought of before the move. If this happens, they may be reluctant to tell you about them for fear of putting you out. Encourage them not to delay telling you when something bothers them. Little problems faced immediately can be dealt with easily with a minimum of emotional upset. These same little problems can turn into major emotional crises if they are allowed to simmer and grow.

This same principle applies to you and your family. If there are things your parents do that you see as a problem, tell them immediately. There is no need to be accusatory or demanding. In all probability, they are not aware they are doing anything to upset you. Remember, the goal is to form a new extended family. Although we should always treat the members of our household with love and respect, we should also let them know when they are engaging in disturbing or unacceptable behavior. Your parents will never be true members of your household unless you approach problems with them in the same way you do with your spouse and children and they do the same thing.

Problems almost never start out as insurmountable. In most cases, they get that way because no one wanted to talk about them for fear of hurting someone's feelings or getting someone angry. Faced immediately, the problems can be easily solved with a minimum of upset.

Family Involvement

Involve the whole family in discussions of schedule changes and dietary changes that may take place. It's unreasonable for a person to have to cook a separate meal for everyone in the house. If there are dietary considerations, ask for suggestions on how these can be worked into a menu that will satisfy the whole family. I am sad to report that my kids were not horrified at the prospect of giving up their frozen-dinner diet for one made up of freshly made foods. They easily went from not only enjoying home-cooked meals to actually demanding them—one of my worst fears come true.

Make sure your whole family, right down to the youngest child, fully understands any physical limitations your parents have. Many physical problems are not apparent and your family, if left unaware of them, can jump to the wrong conclusion that your parents are being unfairly demanding. My mother could see just well enough not to trip over the dog. It was not obvious that she was nearly blind. She was afraid to turn on the stove because she couldn't tell if the burners were on or not without putting her hand near them. She would ask for things that were close enough for her to get for herself, but which she couldn't see. I noticed people, both family members and non-family members, giving her strange looks sometimes when she would ask me to get something for her. They didn't realize she just couldn't see where they were.

If there are going to be a significant number of daily jobs added to the household schedule, discuss each job and who should do it. Is there going to be more cooking? Maybe one of the kids would like to try his or her hand out in the kitchen. Will there be more trips to the store? Offer a raise in allowance to whomever would be willing to make the extra trips. Since no one person should ever be responsible for after-meal cleanup, work out a schedule that includes all family members and takes outside activity time into account.

If family members start to rebel, don't fall for the line, "Well, they're your parents, why should I have to do more work?" No matter how devastated, or guilt-ridden this question may make you—and guilt-building is the sole purpose for asking it—don't let the asker off the hook by giving in and taking chores away. The answer is simple: You are a family, dealing with a family situation, and it must be dealt with as a whole or everyone loses. They may be your parents (or your partner's parents), true, but they are also you or your partner's in-laws and your children's grandparents. Stress the importance of working together as a family. If you agree with the reasoning that they're your parents and you should do most of the work, the end result is an unhappy martyrdom.

This is a very easy trap to fall into. I have yet to meet a concerned, conscientious, loving parent who couldn't be made to feel guilty about almost everything. Your child catches a cold? You mustn't have been careful enough in making him or her dress appropriately or maybe you weren't giving the child the proper vitamins. Your child has an accident? If you were there, maybe it wouldn't have happened. Hurt feelings? Maybe you haven't prepared your children properly for the outside world. This list can go on forever.

Those of us who are suckers for guilt slingers eventually learn to control our urge to please everyone and take care of the world, but it is not easy. We want our children and our partners to be happy, all the time. Children especially know this and can be merciless when it comes to getting what they want. When grandparents move into a home, whole new and exciting worlds can open up for practiced guilt slingers. Learn to duck and stick to your guns. Don't let anyone in the house avoid their responsibilities because you feel guilty about their having extra jobs. They will survive and they will probably be much better for the experience.

Review

Be aware of the fact that your home and your parents' homes are not the same and cannot be run the same.

Do not be intimidated by the fact that you do not do things the way your parents or grandparents did, but be prepared to make compromises.

Before the move, find out all you can from your parents about their eating schedules and food preferences.

Find out what habits or dietary preferences they are willing to compromise.

Be aware of medical problems that will influence your choice of eating schedules or food preparation.

Expect compromise from all involved, not just you.

Make it clear to everyone that you need to know how they feel. Family members should treat each other with respect, but have a right to discuss anything that bothers them.

Most problems are easily solved if handled immediately and directly. Don't let problems simmer and grow.

Make it clear to all members of the family that this is a family problem and that everyone is expected to help.

Be firm in the face of objections. Remember, if everyone helps, everyone will benefit and no one will be overworked.

Don't give in to guilt over added responsibilities. Everyone needs to be helpful and cooperative.

13
YOUR NEW LIFE

Caring for elderly parents is no different than any other major life change we have encountered. It has the potential for offering us new, deeper, adult relationships. It can also throw us into a situation filled with sadness and emotional upheaval. There will certainly be periods of joy and discovery as well as feelings of sadness and helplessness. All these situations can help us grow and expand if we let them, it's up to us.

Many of the experiences I have shared told of our mistakes. I did this for two reasons. First, we learn much more quickly from our mistakes than from our successes. Quite often, when we are successful at something, we are not sure why. Our mistakes, however, have a tendency to leap out and hit us between the eyes. My family and I made a lot of mistakes in our attempt to build a new home that included my mother and my father and my husband's mother. There are many things we would probably do differently if we had them to do over, but we need to remember that we are human and therefore not perfect. Human beings make mistakes. We have, though, the wonderful gift of being able to learn and grow from our mistakes.

The second reason I shared our mistakes in this book is to reassure those of you who read it that you are not alone. You are not the only one who is encountering unexpected problems in dealing with elderly parents. You are not the only one who gets frustrated and resentful at times. You are also not an ungrateful child incapable of getting things right. You are a person who is trying your level best to help all of the people you love.

Sometimes we confuse intentions with outcomes. We assume if our intentions are good, the outcome will be as we expected. Life isn't like that. Even the best-intentioned plans can flop. We have found that even the flops can be redeemed if enough thought and planning are invested in the whole process of bringing your parents into your home. Grandma McGurn slept with her eyes open. You won't have to sleep with your eyes open if you keep them open while discussing and planning for situations and problems that might arise in bringing two families together under the same roof.

This does not mean that we are looking at the idea of bringing parents into our home as a burdensome task for which we need prearranged escape routes. It simply means we are willing to acknowledge the fact that there may be problems. We also need to acknowledge the fact that there may not be problems. We usually do a lot of planning before we go out to buy a new car. This does not mean we consider new car shopping a burden. We are just acknowledging that it is something important that warrants careful consideration.

Two people I talked to found that after carefully considering their parent's problems and possible alternatives that it wasn't necessary to take the parent out of her own home. They arranged for home health care. The parent was happy to be able to stay in her own home and having a home-health-care worker come in for a few hours a day was enough to handle the problems the parent was having. In addition, the mother was signed up with an emergency medical agency and given an emergency response system in case an emergency arose while she was alone. When this family started discussing the problems their elderly mother was having, they were convinced she either would have to go to a nursing home or live with them. The solution they finally reached was a much better solution in their case than disrupting the mother's life and their own with a move. The important message for them and for you is that there are many approaches to family problems and the best solution for everyone involved can be found if we take the time to consider all of the possible alternatives.

Decision-making

All the people interviewed for this book seemed to agree that if they didn't spend a lot of time thinking about the decision to have parents move in, they should have. Decision-making is important for many reasons.

There Will Be Many Changes. The first of the reasons for conscious decision-making is that there will be many changes made in the family because of this move. Changes can be made smoothly with a minimum of disruption for everyone involved, or they can be made in an emergency-like atmosphere. With some pre-planning and decision-making, changes can be made without becoming a threat to anyone involved.

Make lists of any physical problems your parents have and what changes might need to be made to accommodate them. List every room in the house and decide what, if any, changes might need to be made in each room.

Encourage each person in your household to make suggestions about needed changes. With every person involved aware of problems and actively working to find solutions, those solutions will be much easier to find. If anyone objects to proposed solutions, hear them out and try to find alternate solutions. To start this new life with resentments already in place is asking for emotional disaster.

People Need to Feel They Count. Everyone in your family counts. If major changes are made in your home without the direct feedback of everyone involved, you are running the risk of hurting one of your family members and making them feel less than important. This can be avoided by making sure everyone is involved in the planning and decision-making before the move.

In addition to group family meetings, talk to each person privately. Children will often refuse to voice objections in front of a group for fear of being made fun of or being called selfish. Assure your children that they have a right to their feelings. Seriously consider all objections voiced.

Remind your family that very few of life's problems can be solved with "yes" or "no" answers. In most cases, the object is not necessarily to decide whether or not the grandparents will move in, but how best to accomplish the moving in to everyone's satisfaction.

Planning Helps You Feel in Control. Even if all of your plans blow up in your face, you still feel more in control if you've made decisions and intended to follow a course of action. Since you will be dealing with elderly people who may not be in the best of health, it is practically a given that many of your plans will not come into use. However, the fact that you did plan, make decisions, and take time to consider alternatives, will give you the stability you need to deal with unexpected turns of events.

> When I found myself slipping into a martyr mode, it helped to be able to say to myself, "You were the one who decided to bring Mom in here. You were the one who assured the family that there were no insurmountable problems. It was your decision, now find a solution." If I could remind myself, when things seemed to be going wrong, that this was, indeed, my idea, it helped me to pull out of a bad mood and start looking for constructive answers to the problems at hand. It helped me to keep from feeling helpless. (K.V.)

While the planning will help you to feel in control, avoid actually trying to control everyone. People, yourself included, rebel violently when others try to control them. Make plans, but be sure to keep an open mind about those plans. What seems perfectly reasonable before the move may become next to impossible to accomplish after the move. Don't become discouraged. The ability to be flexible is essential if all concerned are to be happy living together.

Try not to assume other members of your family or your parents will think something is a good idea just because you do. If they object to a suggestion, don't take it personally. Everyone has his or her own likes and dislikes and needs to be able to express them without being made to feel guilty.

The life you need to feel in control of is your own. If you are busy trying to control everyone else's life, you will lose control of your own. Take care of yourself and everything else will fall into place.

Emotional Issues

The emotional issues that arise in moving parents into the home will probably be the most disconcerting and may be the most surprising aspect of this whole venture. Emotional upset, however, can be minimized if some simple steps are taken.

Realize That Problems May Arise. The simple acknowledgement that problems may arise will be a big help in keeping them to a minimum. If we go into a major life change assuming that nothing will ever bother us, we are asking for trouble. People have different personalities, different likes and dislikes, and different ideas about how things should be done. It would be very unfair to expect our families or our parents to give up their personalities completely to accommodate a new state of life. Accept emotional upsets as a fact of life. They are. Try to look at them realistically and not let them become bigger than life.

When problems do arise, take the time to pinpoint exactly what is bothering you about the situation. It's frightening to find ourselves in a fit of anger or depression and have no idea what is causing it. Are the people in your household shirking

169

their responsibilities? Taking each other for granted? Behaving in an unacceptable manner? Are you afraid of something that you never thought would bother you?

Several months before my mother passed away, she had to have a tracheotomy. I didn't really think about it much while she was in the hospital. It was just a medical procedure that was needed to help her breathe. An incision was made in her windpipe and a tube was inserted. This tube was then attached to a ventilator. While in the hospital, the ventilator did her breathing for her. Things changed drastically, though, when she came home from the hospital with the tracheostomy tube still in place. She no longer needed the ventilator, but the doctors wanted to have the opening in case of emergency. The tracheostomy needed to be tended to and her lungs needed to be suctioned out periodically because she couldn't cough properly. I honestly didn't think I would have any trouble performing the procedures they showed me at the hospital. I was wrong. I found myself getting angry at my mother if she asked to be suctioned out. I would remind her the doctors said not to do it too often. The fact was, once was too often for me. The whole thing terrified me. I was afraid I would hurt her. I was afraid I'd get sick because I came to find the whole procedure disagreeable. In the hospital, a therapist had performed the procedure to show me how to do it. Watching and doing are two extremely different things. I also became very confused as to why I would get so angry at her. She couldn't do the procedure for herself. She had to ask for help. I became more and more upset with her and the more I got upset with her, the more angry I got at myself. I had to admit that I just couldn't do it. My husband took over that part of my mother's care. Although he didn't find it a fun job, it didn't frighten him the way it did me. If he hadn't been able to do it either, we would have had to hire a nurse to do it. That, too, would have been a reasonable solution. It took me a while to identify the real reason for my anger in this situation. Once the reason was identified, we were able to find a solution.

This was only one of hundreds of emotional issues we had to face and deal with. Remember, though, in our case, my mother was suffering from a severe chronic degenerative disease. Ours was not necessarily a typical situation. Since there was no hope that my mother would recover, we did face emotional issues not present in most other homes. Although we never expected all of the emotional twists and turns that did occur, we were, at least, open to the idea that there might be emotional issues to deal with. From that base, we were able to deal with problems that did arise, expected or not.

Face Each Problem as It Arises. Try not to ignore emotional problems. This will only make them last longer. Face them for what they are—another part of normal life. Don't deny that they are there. You will be calling yourself a liar. This can only hurt you.

I began to resent the fact that my mother depended solely on me for entertainment. She didn't seem to have any friends. I would feel guilty every time I went out with my friends. She complained about being bored and having nothing to do. She didn't seem to want to do anything with anyone but me. These feelings of guilt and resentment kept building up until I no longer enjoyed myself when I went out. I would get a knot in my stomach before I ever went out. Finally, I brought this subject up at an ACOA meeting. I was told that I wasn't totally responsible for keeping my mother entertained. It was suggested that I take her to a senior center in our area and arrange for her to use their transportation system. I did what I was told. The senior center has many activities and although I am more than willing to drop her off and pick her up, she can also call and a minibus will come and get her. This means she doesn't need me to be available for her to get there. Although she seemed very reluctant, she agreed to sign up for a class at the center. I think once she starts to get involved, she will find she enjoys it. (K.V.)

Don't Create Problems. Creating problems can be just as dangerous as ignoring them. Don't try to solve problems that don't exist. We all have a tendency, especially during difficult times, to project into the future. We begin to think, if things are bad now, what will they be like in a year from now, or two years from now? This kind of thinking can only send us into a black hole of depression, and will most certainly keep us from enjoying today. We can make reasonable plans for the future. We can learn from the mistakes of the past. But, if we are to remain sane and healthy, we must live in the present. If we encounter a problem today, we should do whatever we can today to deal with the problem, and then let it go. Tomorrow will take care of itself. It is today that needs tending to.

Like Jane (J.M.), I agonized over my mother's failing health. I was not so much afraid that she would die, but that she would have to go to a nursing home. At the same time, my husband was agonizing over the idea that I would refuse to put my mother in a nursing home and we would be tied to her health problems for years to come. We both created our own problems by dwelling on possible future catastrophes. As it turned out, both of us worried about decisions we would never be called on to make. This is usually what happens when we ignore today and focus on problems that may or may not happen in the future.

Try Not to Become Isolated. It is very easy to shrink your world to include only your immediate family and your parents. This can be very dangerous. People need people. The people who live in a house together are often not able to help other family members because they are too close to the problems at hand. Find the time to socialize with your friends. Encourage your parents to socialize with their friends. Make yourself make time for your social needs. If you don't, you are running the risk of becoming overwhelmed and understimulated.

Get All the Help you Can. Being "strong" and "brave" only works in the movies. There is no doubt that the new living conditions set up by bringing your parents into your home will, at times, be stressful. Find people you can talk to about it. Find people who can come in and take over for you when you need a break. Without help, it is very easy to break down both physically and emotionally. If this happens, you will be of help to no one. Do everyone involved a favor—don't stand alone on your own two feet. Jane (J.M.) contacted an Alzheimer's support group, Karen (K.V.) went to AA and Adult Children of Alcoholics for help. They were not showing weakness by asking for help. They were, in fact, being very brave. It sometimes takes more courage to ask for help than to quietly wither away. There is support for us if we look for it.

The American Association of Retired Persons (AARP) has published several pamphlets on caregiving in the home. Some of these include: *A Path for Caregivers, Home is Where the Care Is, Long-term Care, The Right Place at the Right Time: A Guide to Long-Term Care,* and *A Handbook About Care In the Home: Information on Home Health Services.* These and other helpful pamphlets can be obtained by writing to the American Association of Retired Persons, 1909 "K" Street N.W., Washington, DC 20049, or by calling your local AARP office. In addition, most hospitals today offer at least some guidance in geriatric care. Call your local hospital and find out what services are offered and how to go about receiving the services you think you or your parent would benefit from. If there are any nursing or retirement homes in your area, contact them to find out if they offer services for non-resident seniors in the area; many do. Finally, many churches now have senior clubs and offer some in-home help with the elderly.

Use every resource at your disposal. Expand your world and that of your parents. Become reacquainted with your extended family. I have always been the type of person who felt I could handle anything that happened on my own. Strong. Tough. I was the one others came to for help. I didn't need help. How wrong I was. I learned through the extended family that grew because my parents lived with us that doing things on your own isn't the best way. Alone you can become overwhelmed and break down. If, on the other hand, you ask for help and accept it with love, you will look around yourself one day and find a wonderful thing has happened—a new, bigger, more loving and helpful family has been created—a family that is there for you in times of need and also there for you in times of triumph. What a wonderful gift for my parents to have given us! It probably would never have happened if my mother's need hadn't caused her to accept our help. In helping her, we learned how to accept help. And the circle continues even though she is gone.